About this b

Marketing Learning in Sports, Leisure and Recreation is one of a new series of guides from the Campaign for Learning. The author explains how marketing principles can be used to develop, promote and deliver learning in a number of sectors. Although the focus of the books is on marketing learning provision, many of the common sense recommendations apply to the complete range of products and services offered by many community venues.

Each guide introduces the key marketing concepts and approaches for a non-specialist audience and adds case studies, research and applications to show how learning can be best promoted in practice. The books draw on the Campaign's extensive experience of promoting learning in different sectors with a wide range of partners.

The series is aimed at anyone interested in marketing learning in all its forms to a wider audience, with separate titles covering the following sectors:

- *Marketing Learning in Sports, Leisure and Recreation*
- *Marketing Learning in Arts, Culture and Heritage*
- *Marketing Learning in the Workplace*

Who should read this book?

You may be:

- a marketing professional working in a sports, leisure and recreation venue;
- an education officer working in a sports, leisure or recreation venue;
- working to widen participation in learning and/or sports and leisure for a local council or a Learning and Skills Council;
- working for a learning provider and interested in new ways to engage your audience;
- or simply interested in tapping into people's natural interest in sports, leisure and recreation.

Understanding Your Learning Audience: a summary of five years' qualitative research into learning attitudes is a companion volume to the Marketing Learning series. The book looks behind the statistics to explore attitudes to learning of family members, older people and young people not participating in learning. Attitudes of employers and managers to workplace learning are also covered.

About the Campaign for Learning

The Campaign for Learning is a national charity which aims to stimulate learning that will sustain people for life. It works in three main areas – workplace learning, family and community learning and learning to learn in schools – and it co-ordinates Family Learning Week and Learning at Work Day each year. It also carries out research, advocacy and demonstration projects in the cause of learning.

The Campaign is supported by the Learning and Skills Council, a wide range of public and private organisations, voluntary sector organisations and individuals.

Contents

Introduction

If we can be sure of one thing, it is that the 21st century will be one of change and that the ability to learn and adapt will be the best insurance that anyone can have against insecurity, in or out of work.
(The Learning Age, Department for Education and Employment, 1998)

Why promote learning?

This guide will help you attract more people to your venue to learn, and in particular those who might not normally participate. The Campaign's experience in working with a range of partners in the sports, leisure and recreation sectors has shown that it is an extremely effective way of engaging the interest and motivation of those least likely to participate in other forms of learning. Engaging these groups is essential, both for them as individuals and for society as a whole, and numerous research studies have consistently shown the social, health and economic benefits of learning.

As this guide constantly shows, learning is not just about courses or qualifications. Often the learning people do at your venue will be informal; for example, swimming, using the gym, following a hobby, or simply spending time together with their families and friends. At the same time this guide will help you assist your visitors to develop their interests more formally, whether through courses, groups or self-study. Such formal learning will not only help them improve faster, but can also help build their confidence and interest to participate in learning for a qualification, with all the added benefits that this brings.

Helping people take those first steps back into learning will mean thinking about a range of factors, from how you advertise your service, to providing information and advice in the right way at the right time. It also looks at forming partnerships with local learning providers who can help you and your audience. This guide sets out practical advice on these and other issues to help you market learning in sports, leisure and recreation.

Do people want to learn?

When it comes to marketing learning, we can often assume that we need to persuade individuals to do something they find inherently distasteful. However, we are all born enthusiastic and highly effective learners. Most children have learnt half of their vocabulary by the time they are six. Toddlers can drive their parents to distraction with the constant stream of 'why' questions which they use to learn about the world. We are all natural learners.

So why aren't adults flocking to enrol on courses or to use sports, leisure and recreation facilities more readily?

In simple terms, learning as an adult does not replicate the free-form, joyful experience of learning as a young child as adults have other priorities. They have also had a minimum of eleven years formal education, which, in many cases, defines their expectations of learning for the rest of their lives. A tangled web of barriers to learning builds up over the years that can overwhelm an individual's learning motivation. The Campaign for Learning's publication *Understanding Your Learning Audience*, published as a companion resource for this guide, analyses individuals' barriers and motivation for learning in more detail.

All is not lost, however. Research has shown that, given the right circumstances, an enthusiasm for learning can be restored. The Campaign for Learning's qualitative research into attitudes to learning amongst adults not currently learning has found that although most respondents initially relate learning to their school experiences, a more developed discussion normally reveals that learning is already part of their everyday life (See *Understanding Your Learning Audience*). We really do 'learn something new every day'.

Indeed, many adults harbour a secret desire to learn about something that fascinates them. Topics of unsatisfied curiosity mentioned in focus groups include subjects such as Marine Biology, Sports Coaching and Egyptology. Sadly, these learning ambitions are normally qualified with statements such as: 'But I could never spare the time or money to do that'.

What do we mean by learning?

There is evidence that a latent desire to learn exists in far more adults than are currently participating in the formal adult education system. It is not fear of the unknown that is stopping them learning. They have a clear expectation of what

case study

Getting the footie scores, right now!

Mobile phone company Orange has tapped into people's natural curiosity with its 'Learn' advertising campaign, which offers anyone free training in how to use their phone better. Orange had come to realise not just that the technology was outstripping people's knowledge of how to use it, but that people are fascinated by learning itself and would trust a brand which offered them opportunities to do it. So, Orange has created an entire curriculum, which offers learners choice over what and how they learn. For example, a customer interested in football will be taught how to download scores using WAP, while many Orange shops now offer interactive learning games for those who prefer a more hands-on approach than simply pressing the buttons on their mobiles. Orange staff are rewarded for teaching people skills, rather than selling phones or products.

learning involves, based on their extensive personal experience. It is an expectation that learning will be hard work and they are not convinced that the potential rewards will justify the pain.

Although the top-of-mind definition of learning for adults not currently learning normally relates to the school experience, most adults will also acknowledge that learning can have a broader definition.

> **Campaign for Learning's definition of learning**
>
> Learning is a process of active engagement with experience. It is what people do when they want to make sense of the world. It may involve an increase in skills, knowledge or understanding, a deepening of values or the capacity to reflect. Effective learning will lead to change, development and a desire to learn more.

Research has identified that adults associate the following words with learning:

experience	curiosity
achievement	widening horizons
self-worth	qualifications
personal growth	skills
fun	knowledge
discovery	
developing self-confidence	

The same research that produced such a wide range of responses to the word 'learning' also indicated that only one in four adults describes her/himself as a current learner.

Understanding this ambivalent attitude to learning is key to developing learning opportunities that will appeal to our latent enthusiasm for learning without creating an expectation of going back to school. Venues that do not feel like a school environment are more likely to achieve this objective, so if you work in the sports, leisure or recreation sector you will have an immediate advantage!

Of course, not all adults are reluctant learners. In 2002 the DfES' National Adult Learning Survey (NALS) reported that 76% of adults aged 16 – 69 had taken part in learning over the last three years. Participation levels were considerably lower among certain groups, however, including: people aged 70 and over (28%), respondents with no qualifications (29%), those with basic skills difficulties (52%), residents of the most deprived areas (67%) and people on low incomes (55%). A more recent NIACE learning participation survey, published in May 2003, found that only 39% of adults aged over 16 admit to recent or current learning.

What do we mean by marketing?

Even the professional body for marketing, the Chartered Institute of Marketing (CIM), admits that marketing is really common sense. The official CIM definition is:

> *'Marketing is the management process responsible for identifying, anticipating and satisfying customer requirements profitably.'*

Not-for-profit organisations prefer to amend the definition to '…satisfying customer requirements without making a loss'. A commonly used phrase among marketers is 'working to meet customer needs'. Peter Drucker, the world-famous management guru, puts it this way:

> *'The aim of marketing is to know and understand the customer so well that the product or service fits him (or her) and sells itself. Ideally, marketing should result in a customer who is ready to buy. All that should be needed then it to make the product or service available.'*

Marketing is *not* just promotion or publicity. In fact promotion is just one of the five 'Ps' that traditionally describe the fundamentals of marketing. They are listed in the box (below).

The five Ps of marketing

Product or service
The product or service must be developed to meet the needs of the customer.

Price
A product or service needs to be priced at a level that is acceptable to the customer and either makes profit, or does not lose money in the case of not-for-profit organisations.

Place
The place where customers consume or purchase the product or service can be critical to their satisfaction.

Promotion
Promotion is perhaps the most visible marketing element. It means communication with customers and can involve corporate identity, branding, advertising, public relations, direct marketing, sales promotion, merchandising, sales and exhibitions.

People
Staff who have customer contact have an enormous influence on customer satisfaction.

The Marketing Plan

Your organisation may well already have a marketing plan. If so, you may need to work with colleagues to review it and consider how it might need to be changed to build in a consistent focus and approach to developing learning.

If your organisation doesn't currently have a marketing plan, your first step should be to research and develop one. The key sections you will need to include are discussed below. More information on how to write these sections are included throughout this guide.

The plan should set out the marketing objectives for your organisation and how they will be achieved. Effectively it will become the route map for your organisation's marketing activity. Marketing evaluation can only be carried out against a defined marketing plan. The key sections of a marketing plan are:

- *Executive summary and contents* The plan starts with a brief summary of the main goals and recommendations, followed by a table of contents.
- *Current situation* An analysis is made of the target markets that indicates current learning participation, types of learning offered by the organisation, other learning provision in the area and local learning trends.
- *Opportunity and issue analysis* A SWOT (strengths, weaknesses, opportunities, threats) analysis of the learning provision is presented, with an indication of key areas that must be addressed. Clear marketing objectives are included.
- *Marketing strategy* A description of the marketing approach needed to achieve the plan's objectives is given, based on the five Ps. A checklist is included at the end of this chapter.

- *Action plans* These set out details of what will be done to achieve the marketing strategy, including timescales, expenditure and resources.
- *Financial plan* Forecast of income and expenditure is set out for each action plan.
- *Controls* The last section of the plan describes the controls for monitoring the plan.

A strategic marketing approach requires the resources and authority to take a broad view of all the factors affecting the success of the marketing plan and you may need to think carefully about whom you will need to work with within the organisation to ensure that you have that authority and organisation-wide 'buy in' to the plan. Focusing all efforts on just one element of the plan, most commonly the promotion, will not result in an approach that meets customer needs; all elements of the marketing plan need to be considered.

Marketing Strategy — Checklist 1

- ✓ *Target market (or audience):* clear description of who the learning provision is for.
- ✓ *Learning provision:* description of the range of learning on offer.
- ✓ *Positioning:* description of what differentiates learning provided by the organisation from other learning (or sports and leisure activities) available locally.
- ✓ *Price:* description of the pricing policy and how it relates to the target market's ability to pay.
- ✓ *Place:* description of where the learning will be provided.
- ✓ *Promotion:* details of the communication plan that will promote the learning provision.
- ✓ *Market research:* description of how research will inform the ongoing development of the learning provision.

Chapter Summary

The chapter discusses whether individuals want to learn and the definition of learning. Marketing is also defined and the key stages of a Marketing Plan are introduced. A Checklist for developing a Marketing Strategy is provided. The chapter concludes with a MindMap™ detailing the key points.

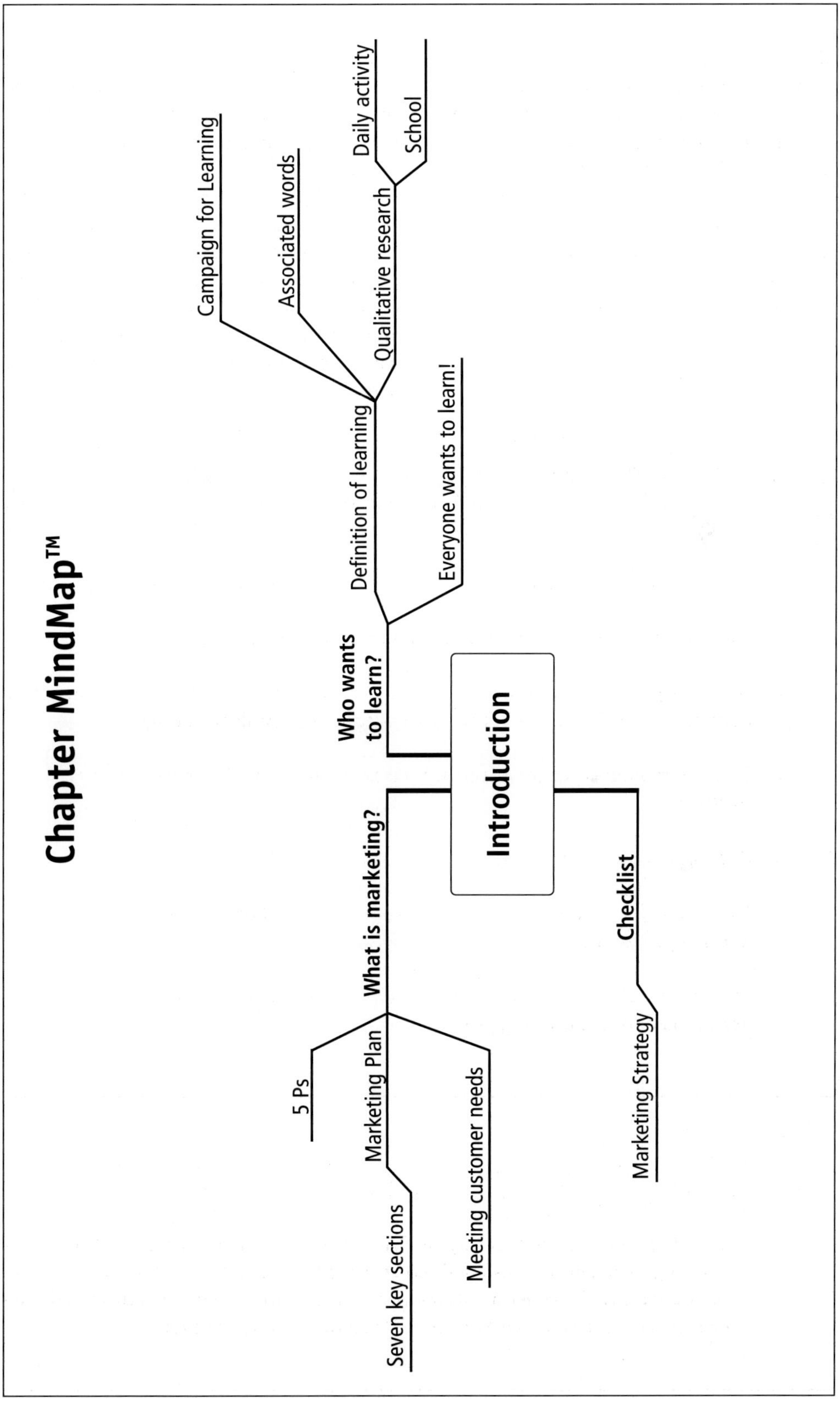
Chapter MindMap™
Introduction
Who wants to learn?
Definition of learning
Campaign for Learning
Associated words
Qualitative research
Daily activity
School
Everyone wants to learn!
What is marketing?
Marketing Plan
5 Ps
Seven key sections
Meeting customer needs
Checklist
Marketing Strategy

1 Attitudes to learning

> *There's education, and then there's learning. You're being taught education in schools and colleges and universities.*
> *Older (55+) focus group participant, Southwark, London*

Marketing learning, or 'meeting customer needs' as the last chapter put it, means understanding what your potential audience thinks and feels about learning. This chapter summarises some of the Campaign's research into attitudes to learning and also explains why and how you should consider people's motivation for learning and the barriers that they face in developing your marketing plan.

There are many parallels between marketing learning and marketing sports and leisure. There are, for example, different levels of engagement:

- passive participation – watching a DIY or gardening programme, or watching football;
- low-level participation – taking up a hobby, or playing the odd game of squash;
- committed participation – joining a rugby team or a gym or signing up for a course or a qualification.

A committed participation 'purchase' involves a significant amount of time and is unlikely to be a spur-of-the-moment decision. Another parallel you could draw would be to the way we might spend time evaluating the options before selecting a pension plan. Although pensions (just like learning and keeping fit) are generally acknowledged as a 'good thing', we don't all start contributing to a plan as soon as possible… if at all! The same applies to learning. In 1998 a MORI survey carried out on behalf of the Campaign reported that while 90% of people believe that learning is important to them personally, only 47% had participated in learning in the past 12 months. This shows that our largely positive attitudes do not always translate into action.

Another similarity between marketing learning and marketing sports and leisure activities is that the vast majority of adults believe they already have a clear understanding of what learning involves. This preconception is normally based on the most recent learning experience. When someone has not participated in learning since his or her schooldays, the perception will relate to that school experience. As we attend school during our formative years, these attitudes can be deeply entrenched and are difficult to alter.

An understanding of attitudes to learning in general is a good foundation for developing a marketing plan that will successfully attract customers to your particular provision. The Campaign for Learning has been carrying out qualitative and quantitative research into attitudes to learning for a number of years. The findings from this research are described in detail in the companion publication to the Marketing Learning series, *Understanding Your Learning Audience*. In brief, the majority of people claim to have a positive attitude to learning, although the word 'education' is likely to elicit a more ambivalent, if not negative, reaction. However, as we saw, this positive attitude does not translate into positive action in many cases.

So what influences the decision to participate actively in learning? The factors involved can be roughly divided into two broad areas: motivation and barriers. If someone is highly motivated they will overcome the most overwhelming barriers, but if motivation is low the barriers will stop them learning (Figure 1).

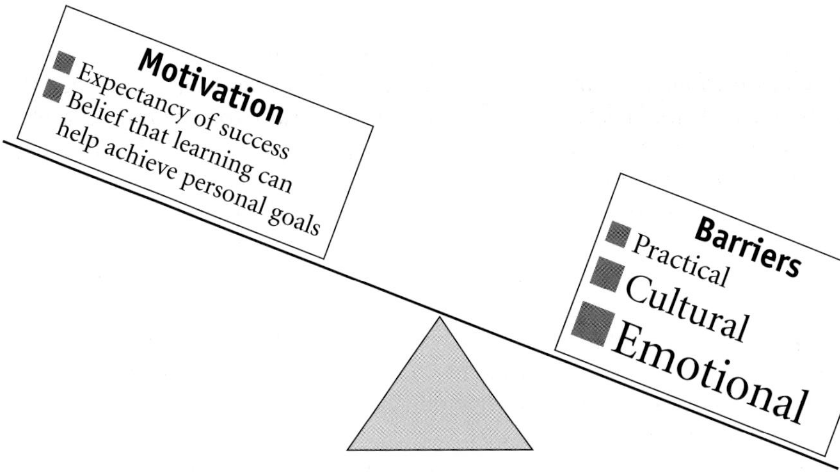

Figure 1: Reluctant learners perceive strong barriers that outweigh motivation

Barriers to learning

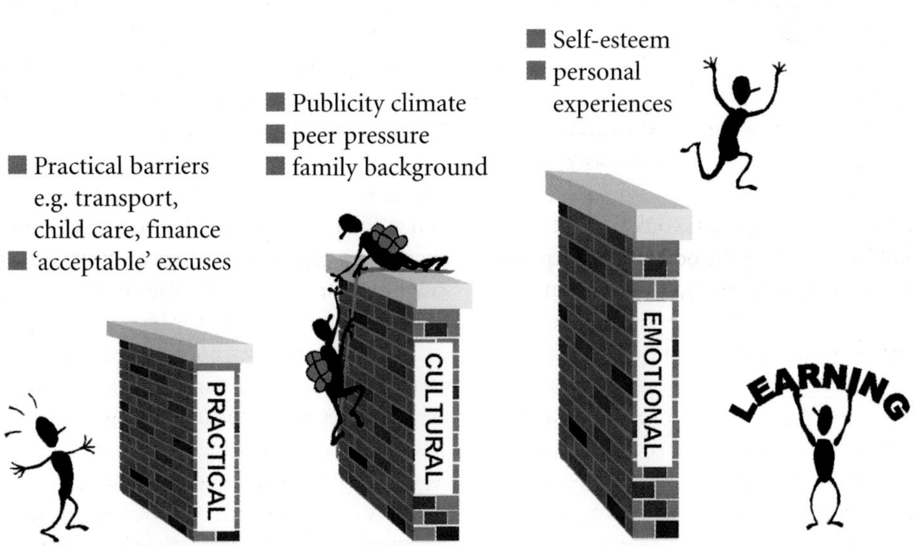

Figure 2: Barriers to learning

Barriers to learning can be usefully defined as practical, cultural or emotional (Figure 2). Practical, sometimes termed functional, barriers include issues such as finance, transport and child care. They relate to the practicalities of getting involved in learning.

Cultural barriers relate to the status of learning in the individual's culture and peer group. Older people, for example, can experience cultural barriers to learning if they see learning promotion that exclusively features younger people. Attitudes of friends and family are critical to the creation, or removal, of cultural barriers.

Emotional barriers are unique to the individual and are created by his or her own personal learning and life experiences. They are closely linked to an individual's self-identity and can run deep.

Research carried out by Partnership 4 Learning (Southampton) in 2002 explored how the different barriers to learning impacted on a variety of audiences. The cultural and emotional barriers are combined in this analysis (see below).

Audience	Barriers
Older people	**Practical:** cost; lack of support about choices; health; care; transport; lack of local access and timings; lack of relevance to their lives. **Cultural/emotional:** 'too old to learn'; no work-related benefit; entrenched in their own routine and lifestyle.
Forces' families	**Practical:** cost; location. **Cultural/emotional:** 'closed family' ethos – not acceptable to step outside the Forces' framework; cultural stereotypes.
Ex-offenders	**Practical:** basic skills needs; fear of loss of benefits; health issues; lack of support. **Cultural/emotional:** learning is low priority; not used to taking responsibility for learning; low self-esteem; fear of not being able to 'catch up'.
Homeless	**Practical:** need for survival; drug and alcohol issues; personal hygiene; difficult to access courses and related benefits because no fixed abode; mental health needs.
SME and retail employees	**Practical:** time constraints; no employer flexibility; family needs; cost. **Cultural/emotional:** low aspirations; employer not positive about learning; low confidence; fear of leaving work environment for training.
Young people	**Practical:** cost; transport; caring responsibilities; poor careers advice. **Cultural/emotional:** peer pressure; gender expectations; negative school experiences; under-achievement; short-term need for money to fulfil social needs; lack of family support.
Women returners	**Practical:** cost; strain on family resources; child care; time constraints; lack of good advice. **Cultural/emotional:** guilt feelings about spending time on themselves; partner may not value learning.

Unemployed men	**Practical:** cost; fear of losing benefits; course availability. **Cultural/emotional:** lack of motivation; low self-esteem; school experiences.
People with disabilities	**Practical:** related to specific disability. **Cultural/emotional:** individuals may not feel comfortable in unfamiliar locations.
Ethnic minorities	**Practical:** cost; also many of above groups' barriers. **Cultural/emotional:** family-led; emphasis on social status of learning; lack of role models; gender issues.

All the researched audiences could clearly articulate a number of barriers to learning, with some local variation. The research found that 'non-learners', who were self-defined, were especially convinced that they faced strong barriers to learning.

54% of non-learners say cost is the main barrier to learning. Only 3% of non-learners agree that course delivery and timings are flexible enough.
Partnership 4 Learning (Southampton) 'Consulting with Learners' Research 2002

It is important to remember that the practical barriers such as finance and flexibility are the easiest to articulate when compared to emotional and cultural barriers. Because individuals feel most confident discussing practical barriers these issues can sometimes seem more influential than cultural or emotional barriers, leading to initiatives to widen participation in learning aimed at tackling the practical barriers exclusively. These initiatives may be unsuccessful if cultural and emotional barriers have not also been considered.

case study

Swapping schools for sports centres to get dads learning

It was as a result of Family Learning Weekend that the Cornwall Adult Education Service's Family Learning team, who are funded by the Learning and Skills Council, hit upon the idea of linking sport with parenting courses for dads.

"Family Learning Weekend 2002 was very successful throughout the county," said Maggie Wright, Family Learning Co-ordinator, "and when we started evaluating the attendance figures, it became clear that a far higher proportion of dads attended events held in sports centres, even if the activity wasn't directly sport related."

Using the knowledge that environment was a barrier for many male learners, the Family Learning team devised a parenting course for dads, held in a sports centre. The course was called 'Don't forget me, I'm a Dad', a title chosen by the tutor who is himself a dad. A sport/play element was built into each session, ranging from an hour in the swimming pool, implementing recently covered parenting strategies, making playdough together to encourage communication development, and a trip to the beach to play beach games and barbecue marshmallows (an important new skill for all the dads!). The course was a great success and another is currently running, with more planned for next year.

Practical or structural barriers are nevertheless real and can be viewed as 'threshold' barriers. They prevent individuals from even beginning to contemplate learning.

Building learning motivation

The Campaign for Learning publication *Understanding Motivation for Lifelong Learning* summarises much of the key thinking on theories of motivation for learning. These theories suggest that learning motivation is built on a combination of believing that learning will bring benefits, thereby helping to fulfil personal goals, and a confidence on the part of the individual that they will succeed in doing the learning and actually get the benefits they are seeking. The individual needs to see a value in learning and have confidence that they will succeed in doing it.

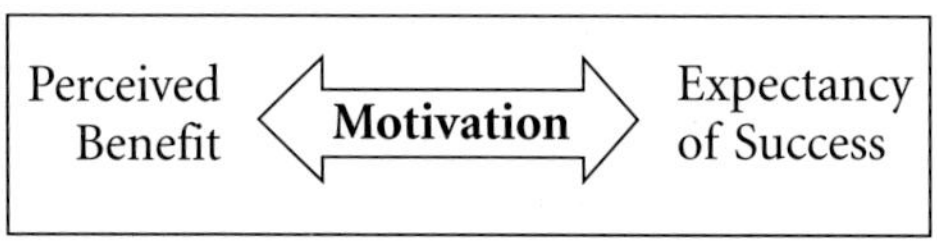

Your job in marketing learning to them is to persuade them on both counts.

The individual's 'perceived benefits' from learning might range from earning enough to pay the bills (i.e. self-preservation), swimming their fastest-ever 100 metres, feeling good as their endorphins flow on a run round the park, being a better parent, or overcoming their lifelong fear of failure to get a qualification (i.e. self-recognition or self-fulfilment). Individuals normally need to satisfy the lower-level self-preservation needs before they become interested in achieving higher-level needs such as self-recognition. For example, the immediate concerns of homeless people are normally related to food and shelter rather than realising their potential.

Learning can help achieve a range of personal goals that form a hierarchy of needs (See Figure 3).

Expectancy of success refers to the individual's perception of how likely they are to succeed in their learning and so reach their goal. Expectancy of success is built on a

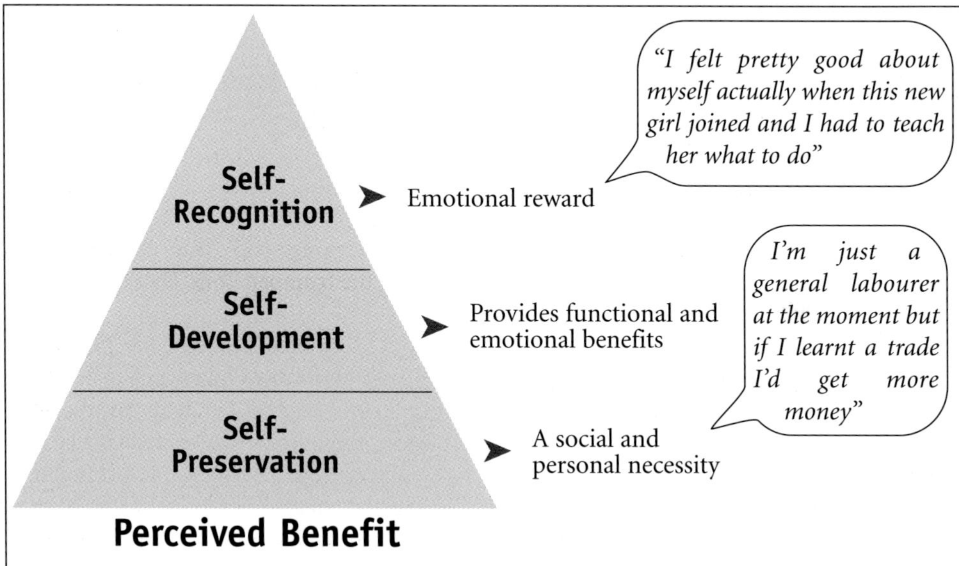

Figure 3: Perceived benefits form a hierarchy of needs

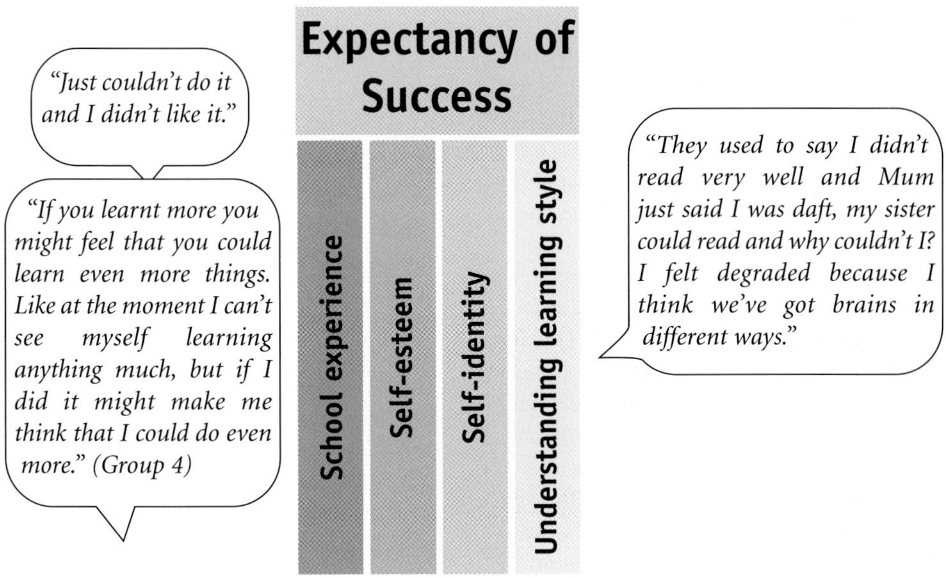

Figure 4: Factors affecting expectancy of success

combination of factors (Figure 4). Previous learning experience is highly influential. And school experiences will be most influential when the individual has not participated in learning since they left school.

Only 8% of 'non-learners' agree they had good school experiences. Partnership 4 Learning (Southampton) 'Consulting with Learners' Research 2002.

It is a truism found in all quantitative surveys into learning participation that those who are most likely to continue learning are those who have been learning most recently. It can therefore be inferred that the motivation of continual learners is very strong. They have become confident that they can succeed at learning and understand how learning can help them achieve goals. In other words, they have a high expectancy of success based on their recent learning experience and are convinced that the rewards justify the hard work.

Reluctant learners must be persuaded that not only can they succeed at learning but that learning can help them achieve their goals.

Only 1% of learners are currently not looking for a course.
Partnership for Learning (Southampton) 'Consulting with Learners' Research 2002.

An illustration of learning motivation

To illustrate the balance between barriers and motivation described in this chapter, try reading the story below and decide which of the three young people is most likely to learn to play the trumpet, Tom, Dick or Sally?

Tom is a fortunate boy, his parents are wealthy and have given him a trumpet and he is extremely talented at music, so he feels confident that he would have no difficulty learning to play. But Tom doesn't like the trumpet and would much rather play the drums in a band. Dick's parents have also given him a trumpet although, unlike Tom, he adores jazz and would love to be able to play it. But he has very little confidence in his ability, and the one time he did pick up his trumpet to learn he was overcome with fear that the neighbours would complain. Sally's parents can't afford a trumpet, but she adores marching band music and believes that if she could only get her hands on an instrument she would make an excellent player.

Which of the three do you think is most likely to learn? Tom, who has opportunity and self-confidence, but no motivation? Dick, who has opportunity and motivation, but no self-confidence? Sally, who has lots of motivation and self-confidence, but no opportunity? The answer, of course, is Sally, whose motivation and self-esteem will surely enable her to overcome all the barriers in the world to do her learning, including the fact that she doesn't actually own a trumpet. Removing barriers to opportunity is important, but without motivation and self-confidence learners will not participate.

Chapter Summary

Marketing learning shares many properties with marketing sports and leisure. We all have many years of previous learning experience and this hugely influences our attitudes to learning. A decision to participate in learning is influenced by a combination of real and perceived barriers and personal motivation. An individual will start learning when motivation outweighs barriers.

Chapter MindMap™

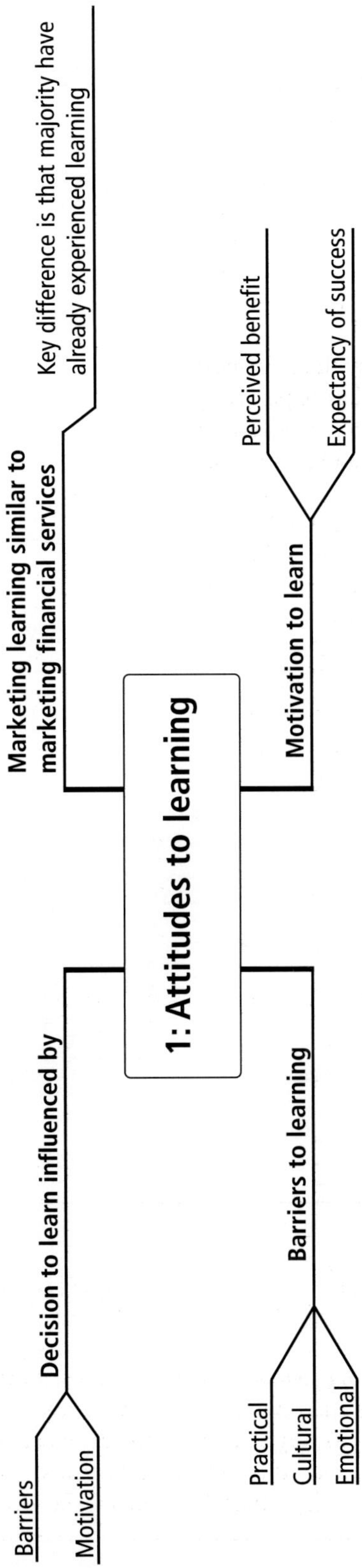

2 Understanding your target audience

> *You can please some of the people all of the time, and all of the people some of the time, but you can't please all of the people all of the time.*
> *(Abraham Lincoln)*

Why is market research necessary?

As Abraham Lincoln well knew, if you try pleasing everyone you risk pleasing no one. This applies as much to learning as any other product or service. Developing a successful marketing plan relies on developing a clear understanding of who you want to reach, what is likely to attract them, and the most effective means of communication to do this.

As you will probably be involved in marketing something that has benefits for nearly everyone, it is tempting to want everyone to participate. There is no escaping the fact that different groups have different needs. A generic product, such as keep-fit classes, can be tailored for a variety of different audiences; for example, pregnant women, skiers or football teams. Not only will the content and the timing of the class vary according to the audience, the most effective means of publicising the class will be different. It is unlikely, for example, that many pregnant women will be visiting the local dry-ski slope, but it is an excellent spot for reaching people likely to go on skiing holidays.

Traditionally, many learning providers have started with an existing product and then tried to work out how to attract a specific target audience or market. It can be much more fruitful to start by thoroughly investigating the needs of the target audience and then developing a product that meets those needs. In the process of investigating audience needs you are also likely to develop a good understanding of which means of communication are most likely to be successful.

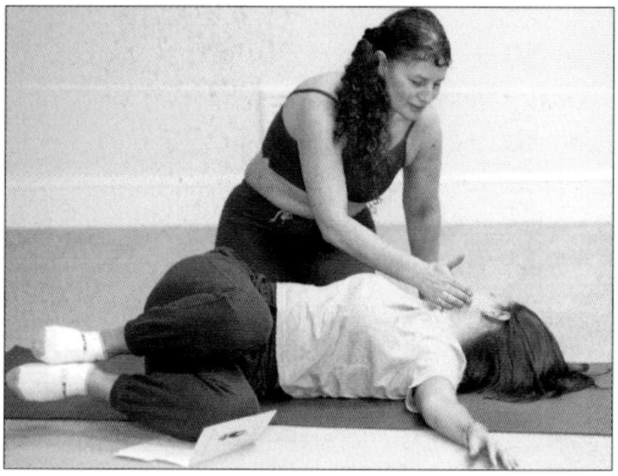

Defining your audience (also called 'segmenting the market')

Developing a clear audience definition can be very helpful in crafting a product and a promotion plan that works. Marketers also talk about segmenting the market to define the same process. Two hypothetical examples are given below.

Mike had been approached by a number of leisure centre users enquiring about first-aid classes. Most of the enquiries had come from young women, so he decided they would be the target audience for the class. He started researching the needs of young women for a first-aid class but became bewildered by the diversity of requirements. Women who worked full-time wanted classes after 6 pm while those working part-time preferred mid-morning classes. It seemed impossible to reconcile everyone's needs. Then Mike realised that all the initial enquiries had come from mothers dropping their children off at the local primary school. When he redefined his target audience as local mothers of primary-age children he not only found a group with similar needs but also discovered an effective promotion route through leaflet distribution at the school gate.

Sunita knew that many of the local gymnastics club members were interested in a class to learn more stretches so she organised a class that suited their needs. At first the class was very successful but after a year numbers began to fall. On researching the reasons by talking to the gymnasts, she found that nearly everyone had now taken the class. When she talked to other sports clubs based at the centre she found that they too had a need for a stretching class. When she rescheduled the class to meet the needs of the other clubs, numbers began to rise.

The importance of clearly identifying the target audience, or market segment, for your learning opportunity cannot be overstated. Defining a clear target audience makes it much easier to develop a learning opportunity that will meet their needs.

Where to start

It can be tempting to start researching local needs without being clear what you are going to do with the findings. The result is likely to be data that raises more questions than answers. Unless you clearly define what you want to find out, the cost of the research may well exceed the value of the findings.

Three Golden Rules of Market Research

1. Define clearly the questions you want answered as a result of the research, especially the 'who' as well as the 'what'.
2. Work out how much data you are going to generate and how you (or a third party) are going to process it.
3. If the research is going to result in action, stakeholders must be consulted before research takes place, informed of the outcomes, and involved in developing resulting action plans.

Where are we now?

Before starting any research, it is useful to analyse what you already know about your current provision and audiences (or target markets). This should help you frame the questions that will be answered by the research. You may want to attract a new target audience to an existing learning opportunity/class, or develop a new class for an audience that already uses other facilities. Either way, you will need to profile your current users and classes to identify gaps.

An analysis of the current situation will involve listing all the current provision and then mapping the participation in each one by a target audience. Accurate data about your current users is needed to complete this sort of mapping. If this information is not readily available you may need to set up a system that measures it over a certain period of time.

Your organisational objectives will influence the kind of user data you capture. These often relate to government or funding-body targets. For example, if you have received funding to encourage older people to keep fit, you will clearly need to capture data on age. Some data categories are suggested below:

Age
Gender
Ethnicity
Home address
Employment status
Disability
Income bracket
Qualifications
Number of children

The table below is a simplified example of how a leisure centre's existing audience uses its classes. It would appear from this analysis that the needs of men over 60 are not being met by the current programme. If the centre's surrounding population were made up of a majority of men over 60 there would be a serious mismatch between the needs of the community and the centre's provision.

% of class from audience	14 -19 girls	14 -19 boys	Over-60 women	Over-60 men
Step class	30	2	10	0
Aquarobics	40	2	30	0
Youth football coaching	0	30	0	10
Internet club	5	20	0	0
Badminton club	10	15	10	15

Table 1

This is clearly a simplistic example. In reality the community's population would be divided, or segmented, into a wider range of audiences. This approach to analysing how well your current provision is meeting community needs can be used regardless of the range of audiences and provision. Your local authority should have plenty of information about the make-up of the local population. Matching the community's profile to the profile of your current users will help you identify target audiences whose needs are not currently being met.

This numerical analysis provides information about the quantity of people using your provision. It is also useful to gather information about the quality of your facilities. You may already carry out regular user-satisfaction surveys that you can use to monitor the quality of your service. The findings can be fed into the analysis of the current position. Chapter 6 has more information about developing systems for monitoring user satisfaction as part of continual evaluation.

Once you have identified the gaps or areas of concern in your current user profile, you can start framing the questions for further research. You may find that a particular audience is not using your facilities at all. The leisure centre in the earlier example would want to explore what they can do to attract more older men. The analysis should help you focus the research.

Developing a research brief

Your research brief should contain a clear statement of the questions you want to answer, using the findings.

Research brief for attracting older men to XYZ Leisure Centre

Figures showing use of XYZ Leisure Centre indicate that, despite the fact that 15% of the surrounding population consists of men over 60, only 5% of the centre's users are men over 60. We want to know:

- Why are local men over 60 not using the existing provision?
- Do they have needs that are not being met by the current provision?

Both barriers and motivations should be explored.

When developing the brief for the research it is important to remember that practical barriers to learning are the most easily revealed. Research respondents need to feel comfortable before they will discuss deeper cultural and emotional barriers, which are unlikely to be revealed using survey methods. These considerations should influence the choice of market-research technique.

Successfully taking action as a result of your research will depend on the support of a variety of people. Both colleagues and community representatives should be consulted when developing the research brief so that they are prepared for action when the findings are reported.

Choosing market-research techniques

There are a variety of techniques that can be used for market research. Factors that influence your choice of technique will include budget, the nature of the information you are researching, and the amount of time available.

Desk or secondary research

This type of research involves gathering already published information and is both cheap and reliable. Sources include national and local government statistics, the media, and reports from trade bodies. The Internet is a rich source of secondary research. The Office for National Statistics website has a large amount of this information, including the data from the 2001 Census. Data relating to population profile, employment trends and local industries can all be gathered using secondary research.

However, as this kind of information is often gathered on a national or regional basis, you may find it difficult to get secondary research that focuses on the target audience in your local community.

Publicly available market research

Central government statistics

The Office for National Statistics (ONS) is the government agency responsible for compiling, analysing and disseminating many of the United Kingdom's economic and social statistics. The statistics covered by the ONS include:

- the Retail Price Index
- trade figures
- labour market data
- Census data

The ONS works in partnership with others in the Government Statistical Office located in different government departments. Each department produces its own statistical publications, and the ONS brings many of these statistics together in its compendia publications and databases. To contact the ONS call them on 020 7233 9233 or look up their web page at www. statistics.gov.uk. The results of the 2001 Census are now included in the site.

A good guide to using government statistics is available from the DTI, in the statistics area of their website, www.dti.gov.uk.

Local and regional statistics

The information that local authorities gather is often available to the public. Area postcodes are a convenient way of categorising local information and can be related to the postcodes of your own organisation's clients to identify areas of strength and weakness. The website www.upyourstreet.com provides a free socio-economic analysis of areas by postcode.

LSDA

The Learning and Skills Council Development Agency is a national resource for the development of policy and practice in post-16 learning and carries out significant amounts of research in this area. Visit the research pages on their website, www.lsda.org.uk to review their most recent work.

MORI

The national research business MORI carries out a wide range of consumer research. Many of their reports are summarised on the consumer pages of their website, www.mori.co.uk.

NIACE

NIACE is the national institute for adult learning and organises national Adult Learners' Week every May. It carries out research, development and consultancy activities in all areas of adult learning. This work is described on the research pages of their website, www.niace.org.uk.

Local Learning and Skills Councils

Local LSCs carry out research to identify their own progress against targets and to identify the needs of employers in their area. The research is often available to local organisations that may also have the opportunity to include their own requests for information. The LSC research department can provide more information for your area.

Qualitative research

This involves face-to-face interviewing of a comparatively small number of people, either individually or in focus groups where complex issues can be explored in depth. Qualitative research often leads to valuable insights that give flesh to the bones of quantitative surveys. It is a good way of exploring the cultural and emotional barriers to learning that are unlikely to be revealed through a quantitative survey.

Qualitative interviewing is a skill that requires impartiality and high levels of tact and diplomacy. Using professional qualitative researchers can be expensive but can help ensure high-quality results.

Quantitative research

This research method covers the questioning of large samples of people to produce statistically significant results. Response choices are predefined, limiting the opportunity to explore responses in depth. Quantitative research is normally carried out using surveys. It is a good way of exploring practical barriers to learning, such as whether the introduction of a free mini-bus would encourage older people to participate. It can also be successfully used for establishing awareness levels of your services.

'Free' market research

Marketing students are often used to carry out market-research projects. As long as the project integrates effectively into the curriculum this can be an excellent way of gathering information about your market. It is not fair to expect the same standard as a commercial market research agency, however. Expectations of the students' projects should therefore be realistic. It is important that a member of your own staff supervises the students' work to ensure that the project progresses satisfactorily.

Buying market research

If you are commissioning research from a commercial agency, the staff should be individual members of the Market Research Society (MRS), the professional association for market researchers. The MRS publishes the *Research Buyer's Guide*, which provides advice on commissioning market research. The Market Research Society can be contacted on 020 7490 4911 or at their website, www.marketresearch.org.uk.

The trade association for market research in this country is the British Market Research Association (BMRA) and they work to represent the business interests of the member market research companies. The BMRA distributes a free Researcher's Toolkit CD-ROM. The Toolkit includes useful information sources and advice on how to commission research. A copy of the Toolkit can be requested by e-mailing admin@bmra.org.uk.

Using the research findings

All over the country there are market research reports that have been read, discussed and then ignored. If the aims of the research were clearly defined from the start, the findings should suggest a concrete course of action.

case study

How a community audit can lead to success

Patrick Barber is the centre manager at Cheetwood Community and Sports Centre in one of the deprived areas of Manchester, delivering sports and leisure learning to meet the needs of the local community. His centre runs taster sessions, coaching courses, has a créche, a computer room and helps individuals work towards vocational qualifications and future employment.

The courses the centre offers and the content of those courses is developed to meet the needs of the community as a whole and the individual needs of specific groups within the community who may be particularly disadvantaged or excluded. A community audit that was carried out by the SRB and the local council helped identify the needs and wants of the local people and the benefits to them of sports and leisure provision.

Before any new course or facility is launched at the Cheetwood Centre it is compared against the findings of the audit to make sure it is in line with what local people are looking for. Short, one-off tasters are then run to gauge the interest of participants before the full course is developed and run.

Patrick says, "The need to understand community need is paramount. No longer are communities willing to be pulled into any form of education by aggressive marketing on behalf of educational institutions that are competing merely to fill places. Communities at present are now empowered enough to make their own decisions on what learning they want to receive and how they want to receive it. Regeneration and community development go hand-in-hand in being able to bring individuals together within communities to assess need and then act accordingly. It's too traditional and draconian to say to communities 'this is what we have, come and use it'. The ethos is to ask, 'what do you want', and let's see if we can provide it."

In most cases any action resulting from the research will require the commitment of a range of colleagues. A meeting to present and discuss the findings should help prepare the ground for new initiatives. You may also want to invite representatives from the community, in particular from any new target audiences. Often research findings raise further questions that community representatives may be able to answer. Use the briefing meeting as an opportunity to engage colleagues in suggesting how the organisation can respond to the research. Concluding the briefing meeting with a clear summary of the next steps will ensure that everyone knows how the findings will be actioned.

Publishing research about your services is an excellent public relations opportunity. Your local newspaper or radio station may well be interested in research results that reveal some new information about the community.

Carrying out market research can raise expectations of improvement in delivery among your customers. Make sure you let them know how you are using the research findings and what difference it will make.

It can be very helpful to test your ideas with the target audience before launching any new provision. Taster sessions out in the community are one way of doing this. The research may highlight the need for adapting the support or conditions of existing provision, rather than developing entirely new provision. Again, testing your ideas with the target audience will help ensure that you implement the research in the best way to meet their needs.

Your customers' needs will change over time, so research needs to be a continuous process. Setting up evaluation systems, as described in Chapter 6, will ensure that you continue to understand your audience in the future.

Survey Methods — Checklist 2

There are many different ways of surveying people's opinions. Each has its own advantages and disadvantages. Some of the different methods are listed below.

	User surveys	
Advantage	•	Can provide opinions from all, or a sample of, the users of a facility.
Disadvantage	•	Do not include opinions of non-users, which may be critical.
	Telephone surveys	
Advantage	•	Can be carried out quickly and cheaply.
Disadvantage	•	Limited to listed telephone owners.
	House-to-house surveys	
Advantage	•	Can easily tailor the sample to a desired catchment area.
Disadvantages	•	Time-consuming.
	•	Not always easy to find people in.
	•	Not easy to interview individual or specific members of household.
	•	One person may be selected to answer on behalf of others.
	Postal surveys	
Advantage	•	Relatively easy and cheap to perform.
Disadvantages	•	Typically low response rate – a response rate of 5% would be considered very good. An incentive such as a chance to win a free day pass to your centre can encourage responses.
	•	Cost of postage can be high but this can be overcome by delivering the survey by hand, perhaps relying on volunteers.
	•	Blind/partially sighted people may be excluded.
	•	Questionnaire needs to be very well written (no interpreter).
	Street surveys	
Advantage	•	Can be carried out easily, quickly and cheaply.
Disadvantage	•	Difficult to control the sample.
	Syndicated surveys	
Advantage	•	Can help reduce costs by sharing the survey findings with other clients. This category includes omnibus surveys (which cover a nationwide cross-section of the population), syndicated package surveys (where the results of the survey are sold to clients when the work is completed), and continuous surveys that monitor performance over time.
Disadvantage	•	The space for information that relates specifically to your questions may be limited.

Survey Questions — Checklist 3

The usefulness of your research will depend very much on the questions you ask. It will be helpful to bear the following points in mind when you are drafting your survey.

- ✓ Begin by explaining the purpose of the research.
- ✓ Think about the order of questions. Try to give them a logical flow.
- ✓ Keep the questionnaire as short as possible. Unmanageable questionnaires get thrown away. Ideally, postal surveys should not cover more than two sides of A4 paper.
- ✓ Do not ask questions that are likely to offend people: bear in mind that the survey may be completed by someone from a different background than your own.
- ✓ Avoid ambiguous questions.
- ✓ Keep the wording simple, where possible. Try to avoid using jargon.
- ✓ Be consistent in the terms you use. Don't use different phraseology in different questions.
- ✓ When drafting the questions, think about how the responses will be coded. Make sure you do not include questions that generate answers which will not fit into the subsequent analysis. For example, open questions will generate more interesting answers than closed questions, but will you be able to analyse the information?
- ✓ Try not to present choices too starkly. This tends to make people agree rather than disagree. This is known as the acquiescence factor.
- ✓ Include a box at the end for general comments.
- ✓ Always check your survey with a selection of test respondents before using it.

Chapter Summary

The chapter discusses the key issues central to understanding your target audience. It emphasises the importance of market research and shows the different ways of collecting data and the key agencies involved. Three golden rules of market research are highlighted and checklists for survey methods and questions are provided. The chapter concludes with a MindMap™ detailing the key points.

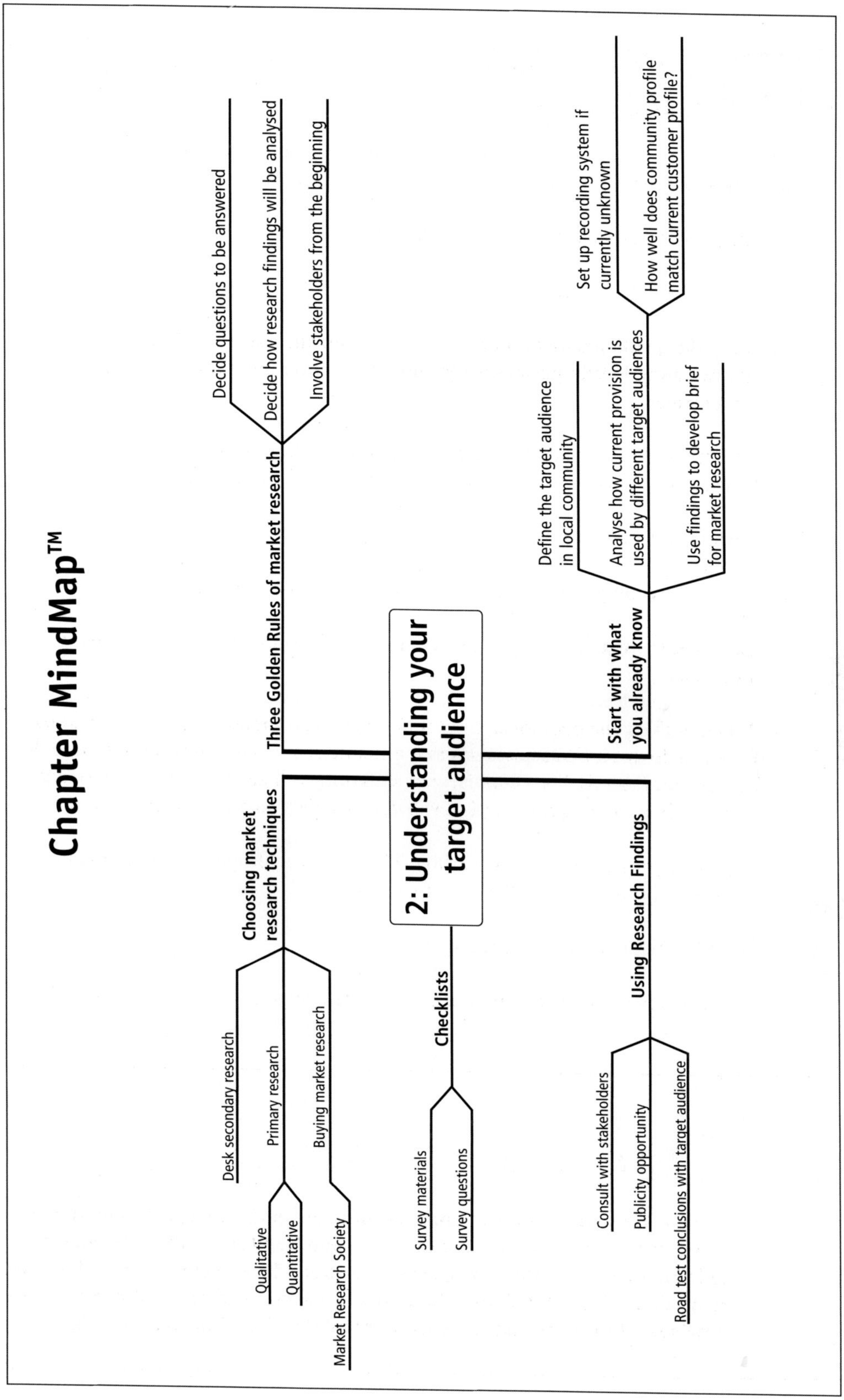
Chapter MindMap™
2: Understanding your target audience
Three Golden Rules of market research
Decide questions to be answered
Decide how research findings will be analysed
Involve stakeholders from the beginning
Start with what you already know
Define the target audience in local community
Analyse how current provision is used by different target audiences
Set up recording system if currently unknown
How well does community profile match current customer profile?
Use findings to develop brief for market research
Choosing market research techniques
Desk secondary research
Primary research
Qualitative
Quantitative
Buying market research
Market Research Society
Checklists
Survey materials
Survey questions
Using Research Findings
Consult with stakeholders
Publicity opportunity
Road test conclusions with target audience

3 Developing attractive learning opportunities

Marketing is defined as the process of meeting customer needs. One of the challenges of marketing learning is that our customers may not be aware of their learning needs. As we grow out of childhood our perceived need to learn has a tendency to become weaker.

As we said in the Introduction, we all come into the world as enthusiastic, competent learners. We need to learn so that we can survive. That spark of enthusiasm still lingers in most adults. Recapturing that early enthusiasm for learning is an important part of creating an attractive learning opportunity.

We cannot rely on enthusiasm alone, however, to attract adult learners. Children's lives are normally structured to leave plenty of space for learning. Adults tend to have more complicated lives that are filled with work and family responsibilities, thereby creating barriers to learning.

Developing learning provision that meets adults' needs involves removing as many barriers as possible whilst boosting their motivation. Achieving this balance will result in attractive learning opportunities.

Overcoming barriers

Chapter 1 discussed how barriers to learning could be categorised as practical, cultural or emotional. Steps can be taken to overcome each of these barriers to learning.

case study

Doubling up on Literacy and Numeracy

The Double Club is an outreach programme run by Arsenal Football Club for schools using specially devised literacy and numeracy materials. The club is co-ordinated by Scott Cohen, a former PE and Maths teacher, and uses teenage volunteers and teachers from participating schools to deliver the programmes.

All of the reading, writing and maths undertaken at the Double Club is related to football and its stars. With football alphabets, pitch co-ordinates and names and events from football history included in the course, the Arsenal Double Club has managed to tailor national literacy and numeracy programmes to meet not only the needs of the pupils they are targeting but the interest of those children as well.

Alan Sefton, Head of Arsenal in the Community, believes football and education are the perfect partners. "I've always passionately believed football can have an influence on educating children. We can make them more interested in learning through the game. So we go into schools and, knowing how overburdened teachers are, we provide them with a structured programme of 'gamefield' materials to make it fun."

Practical barriers

Careful research among your target audience should help identify the nature of the practical barriers that are specific to your community. The most commonly identified practical barriers are time and money. Practical barriers can, however, be specific to the locality. And research in the Isle of Wight found that the biggest barrier to learning was transport.

Funding can be drawn from various sources to help reduce or eliminate class fees. If your audience falls into one of the disadvantaged groups being targeted by government and other agencies you may be able to attract grant funding. See the Resources chapter for more information on grants and other sources of funding.

You may find that your target audience is misinformed about the financial aspects of taking a class. They may assume that learning will affect benefits or may not be aware that some learning is completely funded by the government, such as basic word and number skills, and is free to the learner. A clearly written fact sheet or leaflet with financial questions and answers can help overcome this barrier. The leaflet should be distributed through channels that are likely to reach your target audience.

> *'I wanted to go to the Computer Club with my son but I thought it might affect my benefits. My son brought a leaflet home from school that explained it wouldn't, so we had a go.*

Developing provision that suits the time restrictions of your audience also relies on careful research. As people can find it difficult to commit to a number of weeks, a drop-in approach can be particularly successful. Scheduling classes so that they coincide with public transport can also help. Sundays are good days for attracting working fathers, whilst older people may prefer weekdays.

Child care is a key practical barrier for parents. If providing a crèche is not practical, supplying a list of near-by child care facilities may be helpful.

Cultural barriers

Cultural barriers are created when an individual's culture, peers or family do not view learning in a positive light. Fundamental cultural barriers take a long time to change, but creating a publicity climate that repositions learning within the culture can contribute to that change. An overview of publicity tools is given in Chapter 4.

Perhaps one of the most effective ways of addressing cultural barriers is using role models. Examples of former learners who have come from the same background can be very persuasive. Using tutors from the target audience will also give a clear message that learning has relevance for that audience.

> *'I don't care what Anthea Turner has to say about keeping fit – she obviously hasn't had to face the same problems as my family. What encouraged me to have a go was when Norah, who lives a few streets away, told me how great it was.'*

Holding a class in a location that is familiar to your target audience can help to overcome cultural barriers. If running the entire class is not practical outside of your centre, it may be worth considering introductory tasters in a community venue. Going into workplaces, with the support of management, can help to create a positive learning culture at work.

Family attitudes are sometimes described as barriers to learning. While this may be true, most families hope that their children will do well when they start school. Learning aimed at younger children, but which can also include other family members, is one way of overcoming these barriers. The Campaign for Learning organises an annual Family Learning Week to help build positive attitudes to learning among families. Visit www.familylearningweek.com to find out more.

Peer pressure can be a powerful influence on behaviour. Involving a peer group in the development and promotion of a learning opportunity is probably one of the best ways of overcoming this cultural barrier.

Some ethnic minorities experience specific barriers such as a preference for single-sex classes. Researching your ideas with the community should help overcome these barriers.

Emotional barriers

Individuals may still feel reluctant to learn, even if the learning is free, convenient and comes with the support of friends and family. This lingering reluctance is related to emotional barriers and is also closely connected to motivation.

Emotional barriers can be difficult for the individual to articulate and may not be fully understood as they are often founded on fear. The prospect of learning can create a multitude of imaginary scenarios. The risk of failure and ensuing ridicule can loom large, or school memories of bullying may cause anxiety. The individual may have gone to school in another country and worry that their lack of familiarity with learning in this country will cause problems.

These barriers are deep-seated and have been built from a lifetime of experiences. They can persist even if an individual decides to do some learning, resulting in early drop-out if the right kind of support is not available. Early setbacks can confirm the individual's belief that learning is not for them and make it twice as difficult to engage them in any future learning.

Overcoming emotional barriers can involve one-to-one support from someone who is trusted by the individual. It could be a family member, a friend or a community worker. Targeting this intermediary with information about your learning opportunity can be a good way to stimulate discussion about learning.

The encouragement of fellow students can be invaluable once an individual has started learning. Creating lots of breaks that allow students to interact will support this process.

> *'The teacher at my yoga class was great but it was the encouragement of the other people in the class that kept me coming. They told me not to worry about looking daft as we were all in the same boat!*

Support and encouragement for individual learners is vital in the early stages of the learning in order to maintain their commitment. Allow time for confidence to build before introducing any type of assessment.

Building motivation

Perhaps the most elusive factor in creating attractive learning opportunities is building a learner's motivation. As discussed in Chapter 1, there are two key elements that contribute to motivation: perceived benefit and expectancy of success.

Perceived benefit

The perceived benefit is related to how well the learning will satisfy an individual's needs. If someone feels their needs are currently being completely satisfied they are unlikely to be motivated to learn. It is not uncommon, however, for individuals to discover needs of which they were not previously aware, once they start learning.

'I started doing the keep-fit because I was fed up with being out of breath when I walk up the stairs. There are quite a few dance steps in the class and I have enjoyed them so much that I've started doing salsa – which has come as a bit of a shock to my husband!

According to psychologists, people's needs can be divided into a number of categories. The main categories are listed in Table 2. It has been proposed that the lower-level needs, such as physiological and security, need to be satisfied before an individual is motivated by the higher- level needs, such as self-actualisation and achievement.

Need	**How learning can meet the need**
Self-actualisation	Learning new skills or knowledge can help individuals reach their full potential.
Esteem	Acquiring new knowledge and skills often increases self-esteem.
Achievement	Most learning leads to evidence of achievement.
Justice and fair treatment	Learning about other lands and cultures can increase tolerance.
Independence	Learning can lead to financial, emotional and physical independence.
Belonging and friendship	Learning can provide significant social opportunities.
Security : protection from threats	Perception of personal security can increase through self-defence classes. More generally, the ability to cope with change can improve through learning.
Physiological: basic needs to sustain life, such as food, water and warmth	Learning can provides an ability to earn a living.

Table 2

This aligns with the common-sense view that a safe roof over our heads is a more immediate need than fulfilling our potential.

Learning benefits can either be achieved during the learning or after the learning has been completed. An aerobics class can provide the benefit of feeling physically invigorated during the class but the benefit of increased fitness will take longer to achieve. Feedback from tutors about how the class is delivering the desired long-term benefits is important to maintain motivation. Understanding which needs are motivating learners can influence how feedback is delivered during the class.

> *'Sometimes the amount of work we had to do felt a bit overwhelming but our tutor kept our morale high by explaining how the skills we were learning would help us become better coaches.'*

Contributions from former students who have achieved success can increase the appeal of a learning opportunity.

Expectancy of success

Keeping learners motivated relies on maintaining their expectation that they will succeed. An individual is unlikely to continue attending a class if they don't believe they are making any progress or are likely to fail. Factors that contribute to a learner's expectation of success or failure are shown in Table 3.

One of the best ways to convince an individual that they can succeed at learning is to give them a successful learning experience. The experience needs to be low-risk, low-commitment and highly accessible, with none of the practical, or 'threshold', barriers described earlier.

Taster or bite-size sessions out in the community are a great way of providing risk-free learning that can motivate individuals to do more. This is the principle behind initiatives such as the annual Adult Learners' Week, which includes Learning at Work Day. These initiatives deliver the opportunity to sample learning in a variety of environments. Family Learning Week uses the taster approach to learning with family members in a range of community venues.

A successful taster learning experience will build learning confidence and may lead to progression if the individual is persuaded that this type of learning meets their

School experience	*'I just couldn't do it at school and I didn't like it.'*
Self-esteem	*'I have enough trouble getting the family out of the house in the morning without creating even more problems for myself by starting a class.'*
Self-identity	*'Like most of my family I left school as soon as I could – it hasn't done me any harm. I'm not going back into a classroom now.'*
Knowing how to learn	*'I always found it hard to remember things until I realised that I prefer to take in information visually. Now I use diagrams instead of words to help me remember.'*
Luck factor	*'Nothing seems to go right for me. If I tried learning to swim I'd probably drown during the first lesson.'*

Table 3

personal needs. Maintaining that expectation of success throughout the learning relies on continual positive feedback not only from the tutor but also, ideally, from friends and family. Overcoming difficulties before they seem insurmountable is important to keep learners motivated.

Learning and Skills Council funded Bitesize Intros

Bitesize Intros are free learning sessions that last between one and three hours. They are eligible for funding from local Learning and Skills Councils. Many Bitesize Intros are run throughout May and June every year to provide a learning taster that will motivate individuals to return to learning. Information about the Intros is given to the public on a national freephone number and national publicity normally promotes the offering. Find out more by visiting **www.bitesizeintros.info.**

'I was a little embarrassed, at first, when my family came to watch our self-defence display but I was thrilled afterwards when they all congratulated me on my performance. It made me want to go up to the next level.'

Knowing how to learn

We all learn in different ways. Some people learn well by sitting and talking in groups whilst others find they take in more if they move around or listen to music. Traditionally, school subjects have been taught using an approach that relied on pupils learning by listening and writing. Those schoolchildren whose natural learning style wasn't suited to this approach got a rough deal and they may have concluded that they were weak learners. In reality, they simply had not been taught in a way that suited their learning style.

This kind of unhappy school experience can lead to a low expectancy of learning success in later life, resulting in low motivation to learn. Creating a learning experience that helps the learner discover how they learn best raises motivation by increasing the probability of a successful outcome. Table 4 has some suggestions for integrating learning to learn into your classes.

Encouraging lifelong learning

Once people have started learning successfully, it can be difficult to get them to stop. Every survey into learning participation reports that the biggest predictor of current learning is recent past learning. For example, the National Adult Learning Survey (2002) found that 51% of learners were likely to do job-related learning in the future, while only 12% of non-learners had any plans for future learning. (NALS defines learners as people who have done some learning in the last three years.) Research in Hampshire and the Isle of Wight found that only 1% of current learners were not looking for another course.

Once you have engaged adults in a single learning opportunity, the potential exists to keep them learning. Their learning journey may take them to other providers but their enthusiasm for learning can infect other members of the community, potentially creating more learners for your venue. Sustaining this hard-won learning motivation requires good advice and guidance on the next steps as well as positive feedback on progress to date.

Learning to learn theory	Which means ...	What can be done in class ...
Relaxed alertness is the most positive state for learning.	• Learners' stress levels must be kept low. • The environment should keep learners alert.	• Start with deep-breathing exercises to relax the group. • Ensure there is plenty of natural light and fresh air. Make sure learners are not hungry, tired or thirsty when they start class.
Information is absorbed in three ways: by seeing, hearing and touching or handling – known as kinaesthetic. People normally have a preference for one of these methods.	Roughly a third of learners will prefer to receive information visually, a third will prefer to hear information and the rest will prefer to move around and handle objects as they learn.	• Teach visual learners how to use MindMaps™ . • Use tapes, videos and encourage plenty of discussion for auditory learners. • Encourage learners to move around and use their sense of touch to stimulate kinaesthetic learners.
The brain has an enormous ability to absorb and retain information, but only if the learning process supports the brain's natural processes.	• The brain tends to remember the first and last items in a list best. • The brain loves to make patterns and connections. • Regular review is needed to embed information in the brain. • Emotions help create strong memories.	• Frequent, short breaks during learning will create more opportunities for the brain to remember 'first' and 'last' items. • Linking what is being learnt to events in the news or famous stories makes it easier to remember. • Reviewing what has been learnt within 24 hours is essential to create memories. Without regular review, up to 70% of what has been learnt will be forgotten within 24 hours.

Table 4: Integrating learning to learn into your classes

Information, advice and guidance (IAG) for lifelong learning

Research has found that employers, followed by friends and family, are the most frequently consulted sources of information about taking the first steps into learning. See Table 5.

	%
Employer	47
Friends, relatives or work colleagues	37
Educational institution	12
Media/ Yellow Pages	7
Leaflets	4
Internet/website	3
Other person or organisation	3
Community, voluntary or religious organisation	3
New Deal or JSA adviser	2
Public library	2

Table 5: Sources of IAG which helped learners decide to take the course (NALS 2002)

Once the learning has started, however, the learning provider and fellow learners can take on an increasingly influential role.

Learning something new inevitably widens learners' horizons. A computer club supporting a child's learning can lead to a new interest in the Internet. Introducing opportunities to learn more about subjects covered during a class may help stimulate the individual's next enrolment.

> *'Well, I started in a small way when my son joined the under 11's football squad. The coach encouraged me to get involved by helping some of the boys with their training exercises. He told me about this course you can do to become a coach and now I'm a fully qualified referee.'*

Local information, advice and guidance services can help you provide support to your learners both during and after their course.

Building learning loyalty

The idea of loyalty schemes that encourage customers to return to specific retailers through cash or other incentives were dreamed up by marketing departments many years ago. Green Shield Stamps were probably the first such scheme in the UK. Retailers used these schemes not because they were anxious to give their customers money but because they knew that, in marketing terms, it is cheaper to retain an existing customer than attract a new one. The same is true for learning. It is easier to retain an existing learner than to attract a new learner. While it may not be practical to launch a national scheme such as Green Shield Stamps or Air Miles, you can use techniques inspired by these schemes to keep learners returning.

A core element of any loyalty scheme is keeping track of the members. Make sure that records are kept of learners' contact details and the classes they have taken. Ideally, the records should be kept on a database but ensure you have satisfied the requirements of the Data Protection Act. You will need to ask the learners' permission to contact them about future learning opportunities.

Loyalty schemes use some kind of incentive to keep people coming back. Many of the commonly used commercial techniques can be adapted for marketing learning in community venues. Examples are given overleaf.

Providing a loyalty card will give learners something concrete on which to record their progress. Major retailers use electronic cards similar to credit cards, but a well-designed piece of card that is signed or stamped when classes are completed will work just as well.

Buy one, get one free	Enrol in a keep-fit course and get one class of swim aerobics free.
Collect points for free purchases	Get one activity point for every exercise class – get a free swim with ten activity points.
Loyalty reward	Framed certificate for regular learning over two years.
Recruit a friend	Get ten activity points if you recruit a friend to an exercise class.
Free gift with purchase	Free centre T-shirt if you do 20 exercise classes over two months.

Teaming up with other community learning providers such as museums, galleries and libraries to create an umbrella learning loyalty scheme can provide even greater benefits to the learners.

Recognising achievement

Encouraging learners to celebrate their achievements can make an important contribution to sustaining their motivation for future learning. The admiration of friends, family and colleagues is a powerful persuader and will be given full rein at occasions such as award ceremonies. If award ceremonies are not appropriate, you can stage Open Days or Exhibitions that feature demonstrations of learners' achievements.

Seeing colleagues' achievements recognised and publicised will encourage potential learners or those just embarking on a course. Enter your learners for the national Adult Learners' Week Awards, run by NIACE, for a national boost of publicity to celebrate their achievements.

Chapter Summary

Developing learning opportunities that will meet customer needs demands approaches that will both overcome barriers and build motivation. Suggestions for both are given in this chapter. A discussion of how to encourage lifelong learning is also included.

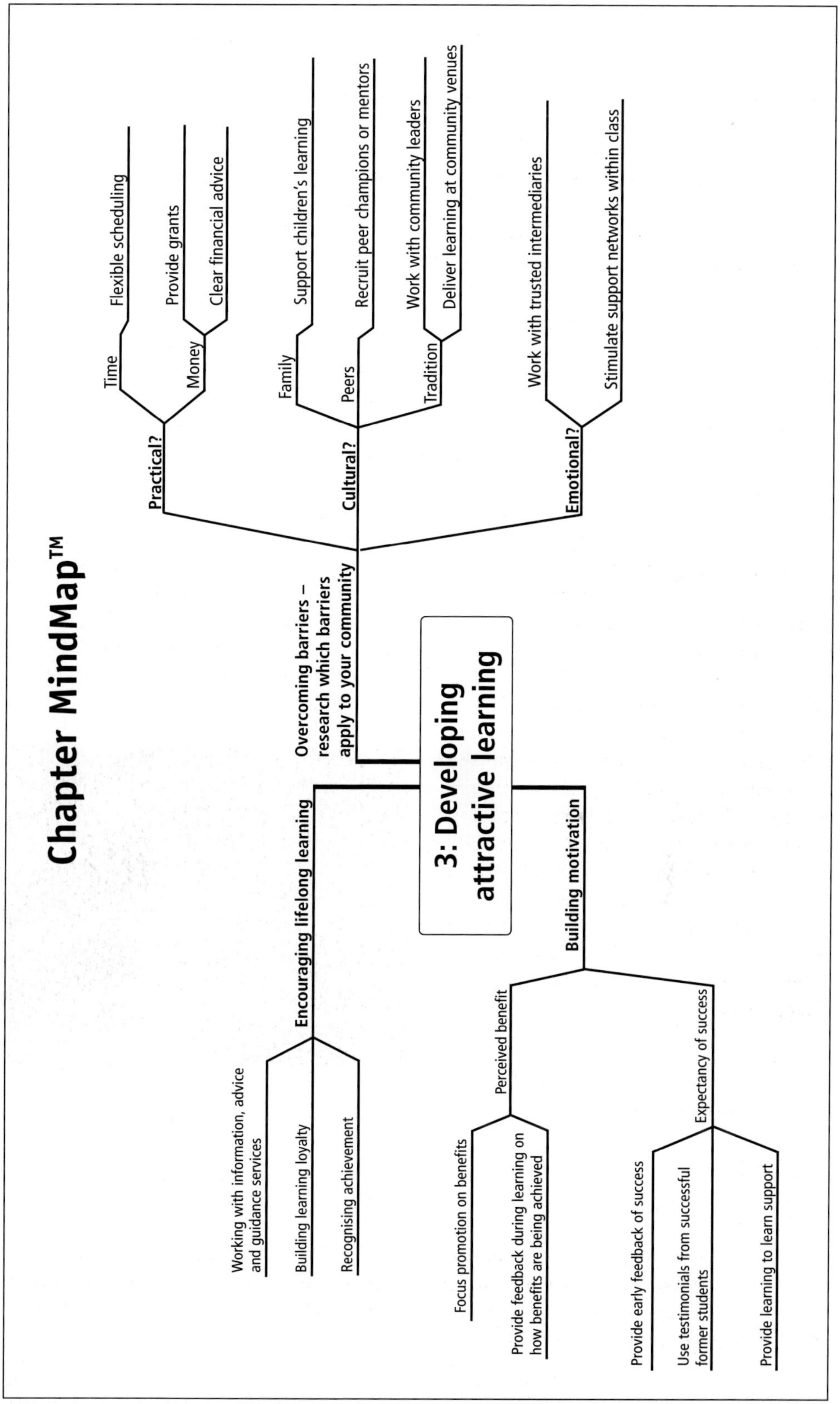
Chapter MindMap™
3: Developing attractive learning
Overcoming barriers – research which barriers apply to your community
Practical?
Time
Flexible scheduling
Money
Provide grants
Clear financial advice
Cultural?
Family
Support children's learning
Peers
Recruit peer champions or mentors
Tradition
Work with community leaders
Deliver learning at community venues
Emotional?
Work with trusted intermediaries
Stimulate support networks within class
Encouraging lifelong learning
Working with information, advice and guidance services
Building learning loyalty
Recognising achievement
Building motivation
Perceived benefit
Focus promotion on benefits
Provide feedback during learning on how benefits are being achieved
Expectancy of success
Provide early feedback of success
Use testimonials from successful former students
Provide learning to learn support

4 Engaging your audience

> *If you do not produce what the customer wants you are likely to go out of business. But, even if you are producing the right products, unless you get your sales message across to the target market you still risk failure.*
> *(Alison Baverstock, Commonsense Marketing For Non Marketers)*

Developing a communications strategy

Before a leaflet is printed or a poster stuck to a notice-board, it is important that a clear communications strategy is developed. You need to be clear who you are communicating with, what you want to communicate, what action you want to encourage, and how you will know when your communication is successful.

Choosing a target audience – who do you want to communicate with?

The target audience for your communications should be the target audience for whom the learning opportunity was originally developed. If your learning opportunity appeals to a wide audience, you will need to segment the audience into communication targets. For example, a badminton class may be offered to all adults in your community but communications to mothers of primary-age children will take a different form from those to young men in their first jobs.

Creating a mental image of the type of individual you want to attract to your learning opportunity will help you identify the target audience for your communication. How old are they? Are they male or female? Do they have children? Are they employed? All of these factors will influence the choice of communications.

Choosing a communications target audience is important because it helps you choose the most effective channel of communication and create a persuasive message. If you try to communicate with a very broad audience you risk diluting your message or choosing weak channels of communication.

For example, advertising in the local paper is often thought to be a good way of reaching the community. While it may be tempting to advertise in what appears to be the more prestigious paid-for weekly newspaper, the weekly free paper will, without exception, be more widely read. Roughly 52% of all adults read a free weekly paper as opposed to the 42% who read paid-for weekly papers. *(The source for this is Newspaper Society Marketing Intelligence Unit, 2002).* It is likely that your target audience will be more specific than 'all adults', however. The age of your target market will influence how effective regional weeklies will be as a communication channel. The 15 – 24-year-old age group are less likely to read weeklies than older age groups. More women than men read regional weeklies, but more men than women read regional Sunday papers.

Having a clear idea of who you are communicating with will help you not only select the right channels of communication but also the most persuasive messages.

Setting communication objectives – what do you want to communicate?

It is important to be clear about what you want to achieve with your communications strategy. Setting communication objectives will help you achieve that focus. The ultimate aim will be to recruit learners to your class, of course. But the decision to participate in learning is normally the result of a long process of decision-making. The communications strategy needs to move the potential learner further along that decision-making process, from a vague interest to a definite intention to learn.

Individuals need to go through three stages of decision-making before they engage in learning. First, they need to become aware that the learning opportunity, and the venue, exists. Awareness is just the first stage, however. An interest and a desire to engage in the opportunity then needs to be stimulated. Lastly, the individual needs to take the necessary action to start learning. This sequence of stages is referred to as the 'AIDA' process: awareness, interest, desire and action.

Awareness

↓

Interest

↓

Desire

↓

Action

Communications objectives can be set for each stage of this process. Your venue may be well known locally but there may be little awareness of your range of classes. A communications objective for this situation would be: 'Achieve awareness levels among the target audience of the range of classes at our venue.'

If there is reasonably good local awareness of your venue and range of learning opportunities, your communication objective should focus on creating an interest and desire in your provision. The messages will focus on the strengths of the provision in order to build a desire to engage in your learning provision. The communication objective in this case would be: 'Achieve a desire to engage in our learning provision with the target audience.'

The final but essential role of the communication is to initiate action among the target audience. It is no good achieving high levels of awareness and desire to engage in your learning opportunity if no action is taken. Communications can include invitations to free tasters to stimulate action, for example. A suitable communications objective would be: 'To attract 30 people to the free aerobics class taster.'

Crafting the message

We are all bombarded with literally hundreds of advertising messages every day. To attract attention, messages need to be easy to grasp with a clearly communicated benefit for the target audience.

Advertising agencies have been researching how to create the most persuasive messages for many years. One of the more useful findings is the fact that we are more likely to be persuaded by advertising that reinforces something which we already believe. Classic examples are washing-powder advertisements that point out children's ability to cover themselves with dirt (an observation which most parents will readily recognise), as part of their sales message. Parents are more likely to be persuaded by the rest of the message as they already agree with the introductory hook.

Positioning – the battle for your mind

One approach to breaking through the fog of promotion messages is to piggyback your message on to one that is already lodged in your target audience's mind. This approach is called positioning.

Scientists have discovered that a person is capable of receiving only a limited amount of information at any time – something the rest of us have known intuitively for some time. So, the amount of information being broadcast may be increasing but not our ability to absorb that information. In fact the amount of information we can retain in our short-term memory is about seven elements.

Our over-communicated minds cope with the avalanche of information we receive in a number of ways. One method is simply to forget things that we decide are unimportant. Another method is to rank the information. We remember the name of the first man on the moon or the largest park in our area. We also remember things that are connected to existing memories. Setting your PIN number to a familiar telephone number uses this principle.

Memorable messages exploit the tricks that our minds use to remember and we can employ ranking to shape the message. If your computer club is the first of its type in your community you have a strong message. The skill of crafting the message is to identify some aspect of your learning opportunity that is being offered for the first time. It may be the first time that a computer club is being run by a group of tutors who are over 50 – a great way of attracting older learners. The message would be: 'The first computer club for the over-50s taught by the over-50s.' An advertising term for this approach is identifying the USP or Unique Selling Proposition.

For many community venues location is the USP. Messages such as 'Your nearest free Internet access' can be strong persuaders. If your venue isn't easily accessible to the community, one of your key messaging advantages is being undermined.

Popular films or television programmes are an opportunity to link your message to a memory that is already lodged in the mind of your target audience. For example, 'Get the figure of those *Sex and the City* girls with their favourite spinning exercise class.' This approach must be used with caution, however, as you cannot imply that celebrities are endorsing your class without their permission. Celebrities normally endorse products or services for a fee but you may be lucky enough to have a sympathetic celebrity living in your community who would be willing to provide a free endorsement of your venue. This is more likely if your learning opportunity targets a disadvantaged group in the community.

Phrasing your message so that it sticks in the mind of your target audience is important to attract the attention of that audience. However, all these techniques are useless if your message is not based on a good understanding of what motivates your target audience. For example, if your target audience are not interested in achieving a TV-star figure they are unlikely to be persuaded by the earlier message for the spinning exercise class.

The Campaign for Learning publication *Understanding Your Learning Audience* explores how motivational messages vary by target audience. Any earlier research that you carried out with your target audience to develop the learning opportunity should also have highlighted what will motivate your audience.

Most persuasive messages will include four key elements:

- a 'promise' or benefit that is desirable to the target audience – often in the headline in the case of print-based publicity;
- a clear, brief description of the product or service on offer;
- supporting evidence/testimonials to lend credibility;
- a clear next step.

Get your bikini figure in time for summer!
Busy local mother of two, Jenny, was worried about fitting in an exercise class before her summer break until she found out about the new *Fit for life* class running at her daughters' school.
'I can't believe how convenient it is. The class finishes just before the end of the school day so I'm always in time to pick up the girls – and I get to have a good chat with the other mothers.'
Pick up a leaflet at the Hall Green or Hamilton Road primary schools to find out more.

The advertising message above has a promise in the headline, a description of what is on offer, supporting testimonial and a clear next step.

case study

Giving learning a sporting chance

To turn potential learners into actual learners, the Living and Learning Centre, based in the GL1 Gloucester Leisure Centre, promoted directly to the local people a fun Family Learning Weekend event of sports, leisure and learning activities. Through informal research with their target audience, they found the best way to reach them was to send publicity leaflets via the local free papers, ensuring nearly every home in the area received details of the event right at their door.

Becky Walton from the Living and Learning Centre said, "Having the event based in a leisure centre made learning attractive to new learners. Another bonus was that people who were at the leisure centre for activities such as swimming or sports were able to attend the event and learn something new."

Eye-catching press releases, highlighting the local angle of the event, helped them secure free coverage on local radio as a news item and in the local newspaper. Attracting local sporting celebrities (members of the successful Gloucester RFC team) helped to generate media coverage and public awareness.

One thing that the Living and Learning Centre might do differently next time round is to record where participants heard about the event. Added to a simple monitoring form handed out to learners, this question can help ensure that money is not wasted on promotional activities next time.

Marketing mix – choosing your communication tools

Once a clear message has been created, the choice of communication method must be made. There are a number of different communication tools to choose from and they are summarised in Table 6.

Given a sizeable marketing communications budget, the choice and mixture of tools can be a time-consuming experience. An advantage of a more restricted budget is that choosing where to spend the money takes less time. If you have no promotion budget at all you will be restricted to public relations and personal selling. In reality, these techniques also cost money when you consider your own time plus items such as postage and stationery.

Advertising
- Print and broadcast ads
- Mailings
- Field marketing
- Outdoor posters
- New media
- Signs outside and inside the venue

Sales promotion
- Competitions
- Gifts
- Tasters
- Exhibitions and shows
- Displays and demonstrations at community venues

Public relations
- Media relations
- Annual reports and other publications
- Sponsorships
- Community relations
- Website
- Visual identity

Personal selling
- Telemarketing
- Presentations at community venues
- Exhibitions and shows

Table 6: Elements of the marketing mix

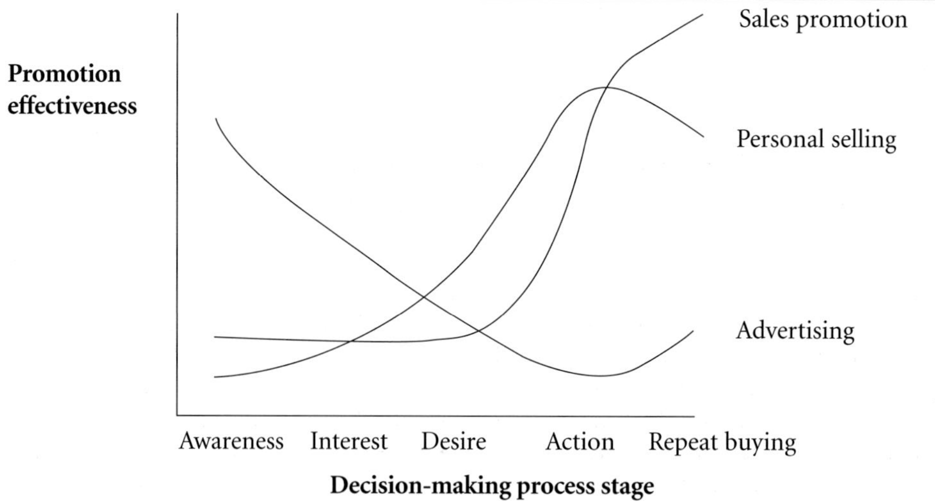

Figure 6: Philip Kotler, *Marketing Management*

Promotional tools vary in their cost-effectiveness at different stages of the decision-making process (see Figure 6). Advertising is most effective at building awareness and interest in your offering. Sales promotion and personal selling is most effective at creating a desire and initiating action. So, distributing leaflets about your latest class is likely to be ineffective if your target audience has never heard of your venue.

Advertising

Advertising can range from the prohibitively expensive, such as national TV advertising, to the more modest costs of advertising in the local paper or on buses.

The most important factor influencing the choice of advertising medium is to determine how much of your target audience it reaches. Another key influencing factor will be your budget. Table 7 gives examples of advertising in different media and the advantages and disadvantages of each.

Medium	Cost	Advantages	Disadvantages
National newspapers	Approx. £10,000 – £20,000 for a black-and-white half page in a tabloid.	High credibility, large readership, timeliness.	High cost, reaches many readers outside the local community, easy to ignore.
Local newspapers	Approx. £1,000 – £2,000 for a black-and-white half-page.	Aimed at local community, relatively low cost, timeliness.	May not be read by target audience, small 'pass-along' audience, easy to ignore.
Television	A month-long campaign in an ITV region (not London) featuring about 80 exposures of a 20-second ad costs approx. £30,000.	Powerful impact, wide reach.	High cost.
Direct mail	Depends entirely on list size. Biggest single cost will be postage.	Flexibility, no competing ad in the same medium, can be personalised to recipient.	Easy to ignore, can be lost among 'junk mail', lists can be expensive to buy.
Field marketing, distribution of publicity material at community locations.	A field-marketing agency will cost between £100 – £200 per person day. Shopping centres charge between £150 – £2,500 per day for using their location to distribute leaflets.	Flexibility, no competing ad in the same medium, can engage recipient in conversation.	High cost if field-marketing agency used but can be achieved using venue staff or volunteers.

Medium	Cost	Advantages	Disadvantages
Radio	A national radio campaign with five opportunities to hear a 30 second advert will cost in the region of £30,000. A regional campaign resulting in 60 minutes' air time will cost approx. £22,000.	Can have high impact in certain environments, e.g. car, local stations can reach a broad cross-section of community.	High cost but lower than television.
Magazines	A full page advert in a woman's monthly magazine with a readership of c500,000 will cost approximately £10,000.	High quality production, can have high prestige, long life, good 'pass-along' value.	Long ad purchase lead time, likely to reach many readers outside of local community.
Outdoor, posters and billboards	A targeted regional poster campaign of 300 panels over two weeks will cost approximately £25,500.	Flexibility, high repeat exposure, low competition from other ads, can be tightly targeted on specific locations.	High cost, difficult to judge if will reach target audience.

Table 7: Example costs of advertising media

You may find that the majority of your target audience watch *Coronation Street* but it is unlikely that you will have the budget required to advertise during the programme, and the majority of viewers will not live within easy reach of your venue. On the other hand, you may be able to afford a series of ads in your local paper, but it may be read by only 10% of your target audience.

Finally, you will need to consider whether advertising will help you achieve your communication objective. If there is very little local awareness of your venue or classes you should consider advertising. If awareness is high but participation levels are low, using a personal selling approach may be more effective.

Most print and broadcast media that sell advertising will be able to give you a breakdown of their readers, listeners or viewers. Bear in mind that they are presenting the figures in the most positive light, however. The National Readership Survey for print media, RAJAR (Radio Joint Audience Research Ltd) for radio, and BARB (British Audience Research Board Ltd) for television give impartial breakdowns of these figures. The respective websites for these organisations provide some information free of charge but detailed analyses are normally available only to subscribers.

Don't forget the advertising media that are freely available to you, such as signage inside and outside your venue. Partners in your local community may provide other free advertising media if they agree to display your publicity within their own venues.

Collaborative advertising
In 1998 a number of organisations providing learning opportunities in the South West of England decided to join forces to promote learning as a concept. They employed the advertising agency ABM, who developed a campaign built around the concept 'One day...'. Television ads were devised using the technique known as 'topping and tailing'. At the beginning of a commercial break a variety of individuals were seen talking about vague plans that they had for learning, e.g. 'One day I'm going to learn French'. The commercial break ended with a repeat ad urging the viewer to make that dream happen now and giving a telephone number where information would be provided about adult education courses. The target of 6,000 responses was reached in just one week.

Sales promotion

Some of the techniques discussed under 'Building learning loyalty' (page 37) also fall into the category of sales promotion. While advertising can offer a reason to participate in learning, sales promotion will offer an incentive. Samples, money-off offers, competitions and free trials are all examples of sales promotions. They can be used to trigger the involvement of new users of our services or to reward regular users.

Sales promotion is a good tool to use for last-minute recruitment to classes. Offering a limited number of free places to users of other centre services, for example, can boost numbers for a new class. If they enjoy the class, they may choose to continue with it once the free lessons have finished.

Personal selling

Personal selling is particularly effective when either you are targeting a reluctant audience who need a lot of support or your learning opportunity is a little unusual and requires some explanation.

Although it may call up images of door-to-door insurance salesmen, personal selling simply involves the personal involvement of one of your staff in promoting the learning opportunity. An example would be giving a talk about the new class at a local mother-and-baby group.

Successful personal selling to your local community relies on a good understanding of the local networks. You should also make sure the individuals involved in promoting your class have the correct information about what is on offer. A pack detailing times, venues and content can be very useful.

Public relations

The role of public relations is to support the communication of your message to your target audience. The difference between public relations and other communications tools is that it benefits from the impartial support of a third party given by the media in which a story appears. It has been estimated that information in the editorial pages of a newspaper is five times more likely to be believed than an advertisement.

Public relations has been described as reputation management, which implies a broader role than supporting marketing communications. It is often used to communicate with audiences other than an organisation's customers or clients. For example, financial public relations targets investors to maintain a healthy share price for companies quoted on the stock exchange. Government relations involve targeting central or local government officials to ensure they view the organisation sympathetically. Community relations aims to create a strong reputation for an organisation within its local community, often with the aim of positioning the organisation as an employer of choice.

In this publication we are most interested in using public relations as a tool to help promote your learning opportunity.

Publications

If your venue produces an annual report or regular newsletter, it can be a good tool to promote a new learning opportunity. If you are part of a local authority, ask their public relations department if any of the Council publications can include a feature about your classes.

Events

Public events such as open days, displays, fairs and exhibitions are opportunities to promote your venue. Be careful not to overcommit yourself, however, or you may find yourself with little time to deliver the learning because you spend so much time promoting it at events!

Media relations

The media is divided into two main categories – print and broadcast – with new media such as Internet and texting a rapidly rising phenomenon.

Although the broadcast media of radio and television seem more high-profile than print, which is newspapers and magazines, the print media do have some advantages over broadcast media. The main limitation of broadcast media is its time constraints. One half-hour TV news programme will contain the same content as two pages of a broadsheet newspaper.

Local newspapers simply have more room for local news than either local radio or television. They are also more likely to focus on a smaller area than radio, and particularly television, so they should be an easier target for your media relations. That said, local TV and radio are likely to reach a far larger audience but many of them will not be within easy travelling distance of your venue.

The most practical use of limited media-relations resources may be to focus on local newspapers to build up local coverage. Make sure you understand how their deadlines work. Most local newspapers have several deadlines for their various sections so you will need to be clear about which section you are targeting.

A press release is a way of attracting media attention. General rules for writing a press release are listed in Checklist 4 at the end of this chapter.

Speeches

A good opportunity to promote new provision can occur if members of your staff are speaking on a public platform. They will need to know the two or three key points about your new class and an easy-to-remember method of finding out more. Make sure details of new classes are promoted widely to your own staff so they can help your publicity when they have the chance.

Community relations

Working in partnership with the local community can raise your profile with your target audience very effectively. This important area is covered in Chapter 5.

Website

New technology such as the Internet is increasing the speed and volume of communications being broadcast and is contributing to our information overload. It can be very cost-effective for organisations that do not have huge advertising budgets. If you decide to develop a website make sure that the address is easy to remember and signposted in your publicity as much as possible.

With an estimated 60% of households accessing the Internet, you can reach a significant audience through your own website. There is a gender bias in Internet use, however, with more men and boys going on-line than girls and women. Other factors such as age and income also affect access to the Internet. It's important, therefore, to create website content that will suit your anticipated audience.

As long as you are aware of its limitations, a website can make a significant contribution to your communications strategy. One of the key advantages of a website is the speed with which it can be updated, although this can be a double-edged sword as traffic levels are unlikely to be maintained unless you are able to commit the resources to update the site frequently. Be careful that you design your site to suit the level of support that will be available.

Visual identity

In the section on 'Setting communications objectives' (page 41) the AIDA process of decision-making was introduced: awareness; interest; desire; action. Achieving awareness of your venue among the local community relies on a consistent visual presentation of all your communications. By using a consistent appearance for your communications you create a hook for your message in your target audience's mind.

If every communication looks different the audience needs to work hard to discover who the communication is from before deciding to accept or dismiss the message. By using a recognisable visual identity, or house style, your audience will immediately know the source of the communication. Assuming your venue has a good reputation, your information is then given some credibility so that the content is less likely to be dismissed.

Creating visual identities is a thriving industry that can charge large companies such as BT literally millions of pounds to develop a logo and supporting visuals for its communications. Of course, an investment of that nature is not realistic, or appropriate, for smaller community venues. You can achieve a consistent appearance for your publicity by introducing some simple guidelines for all printed materials.

Six key visual guidelines

1. Agree on a single representation of your venue's name. If a logo exists, make sure that all staff who are likely to produce materials have access to clean, digital versions.
2. Identify a 'logo zone' for all your printed materials so that your logo appears in a consistent position on printed materials (for example, somewhere along the right-hand third of materials). Ensure that your logo stands out by surrounding it with an area of clear space.
3. Restrict the use of separate logos for different elements of your provision. Your target audience is only likely to recognise one logo – it should be your venue logo.
4. Create a partner logo zone for materials that are produced with partners (perhaps the left- hand third of materials), to try to reduce logo clutter.
5. Create a limited palette of colours for use in your printed materials. Restricting the number of colours will help your target audience recognise your materials.

6. Use the same font for all printed materials. Select a font that is widely accessible to all staff so it will be used for materials produced on computers in-house as well as externally printed materials.

Policing these guidelines can be challenging, but it is necessary to ensure they are followed.

A good way of selling centralised checking of materials is to build the checking into the internal communication process. Your staff can help promote provision through their informal relationships between the communities. They are only able to do this if they know what is on offer, however. All announcements to the community should be made to your staff first, to keep them informed. Before information is fed to staff the printed publicity can be checked to make sure it meets the guidelines. In this way, you can kill two birds with one stone – promoting the provision internally and keeping your materials consistent!

Has your message been received?

It is vital to evaluate how successful your communication has been so that you can learn how to do it better next time. Every communication is different as there are so many variables. The communication climate is constantly changing so what worked six months ago may not work now. Chapter 6 will look at how the development of a customer relationship management database can help you track the success of your communications.

Writing a Press Release — Checklist 4

The purpose of a press release is to attract the attention of the media. To do this you need to supply them with exciting local 'human interest' stories that also reflect what is happening in learning nationally. Here are some general rules, which you should find useful.

- ✓ Head the item 'Press Release' and type the date of distribution.
- ✓ Write a headline with key words. Keep it short and to the point.
- ✓ Aim to write no more than 1 – 2 sides of A4 paper with 1 – 2 sentences per paragraph. Use double-spaced typing and one side of the paper only.
- ✓ Get the complete picture across in the first paragraph – this is often the only part of the release that will be used by the target media. Answer the questions 'who', 'what', 'when', 'where', 'why'.
- ✓ If you include quotations make sure they are recent, accredited and have a positive tone.
- ✓ Use the present tense as far as possible to optimise your story's impact.
- ✓ Avoid the use of jargon or cliché.
- ✓ Keep it impersonal: don't use 'I' or 'we'.
- ✓ Put your most important information first. Only the briefest background information is required in a press release; more details can be included in a press pack distributed later. If the press release is for radio or television, adapt to their needs: e.g. television needs something visual, radio may want an interview.
- ✓ Provide clear instructions about what the recipient should do for more information, to arrange interviews, etc.
- ✓ If the release runs over one page, type 'MORE' in the bottom right-hand corner. Always type 'ENDS' at the close of the release.

Effective Media Relations — Checklist 5

- ✓ Identify who the key media are for your community and who will be your main contacts. Regularly review the media to ensure your contact lists are up to date.
- ✓ Know when the deadlines are for your local newspapers and radio stations.
- ✓ Identify the 'quiet news periods' for your local media. The period between Christmas and New Year is a classic quiet news time, when it is easier to place stories.
- ✓ Research or surveys can be offered to the media to maintain the relationship when other news is not available.
- ✓ Good photographs are important to illustrate appropriate stories. Keep a photo library of essential activities and people.
- ✓ Invite journalists to sample new services, when practical.
- ✓ Embargoes can be used if the media need time to research a story, or if the news needs to break on a particular day; but they should not be overused.
- ✓ If you are using quotes make sure the individual quoted will be available for interview, if asked.
- ✓ A contact name should always be provided on any material sent to the media, including an out-of-hours telephone number.
- ✓ Clashing with major events or announcements by other local venues should be avoided, as should busy news days such as GCSE and A-Level results days.
- ✓ A photographer should be commissioned for major events – don't rely on staff's snapshots to capture an unrepeatable event.

Creative Persuasive Advertising Checklist 6

- ✓ Put a promise in the headline.
- ✓ Stress benefits.
- ✓ Write in language that has visual impact to stimulate images in the audience's mind.
- ✓ Link the first sentence to the headline.
- ✓ Don't waffle.
- ✓ Address your audience directly with a friendly everyday style. Use 'you'.
- ✓ Avoid long words when short ones will do the same job.
- ✓ Offer an incentive.
- ✓ Demonstrate the benefits that come from responding.
- ✓ Show clearly how to respond.

Designing Persuasive Brochures and Leaflets — Checklist 7

The front page:

- ✓ Make a strong promise, benefit or offer.
- ✓ Use an illustration that is directly relevant to the promotion, promise or offer.

Inside pages:

- ✓ Use the inside pages to develop the promise, benefit or offer.
- ✓ Use captioned illustrations and graphics to make a positive contribution to the message.
- ✓ Number the pages.
- ✓ Trail the reply element in several strategic places throughout the copy.

Text, content and style:

- ✓ Use paragraphs and sub-headings to break up the text.
- ✓ Use plain English.
- ✓ Avoid generalisations.
- ✓ Use a mixture of short and long sentences.
- ✓ Get someone else to check your text – ideally a member of your target audience.
- ✓ Check carefully, especially telephone numbers, dates, times and website addresses.

Reply element:

- ✓ Make the reply element highly visible and clearly laid-out.
- ✓ Design the reply element as a mini-ad in its own right, with headline and benefits.
- ✓ If possible, use Freephone or Freepost to stimulate response.

Chapter Summary

Creating a clear communications strategy that defines the target audience, messages and communications objectives is essential to communicate effectively. A good message will have four key elements and should be informed by research with the target audience. Wide ranges of communication tools are available. Choice of communications channel is influenced by who reads, listens to or views the channel, the stage of the communication process and the budget. Communications should be monitored to establish which approaches are most successful.

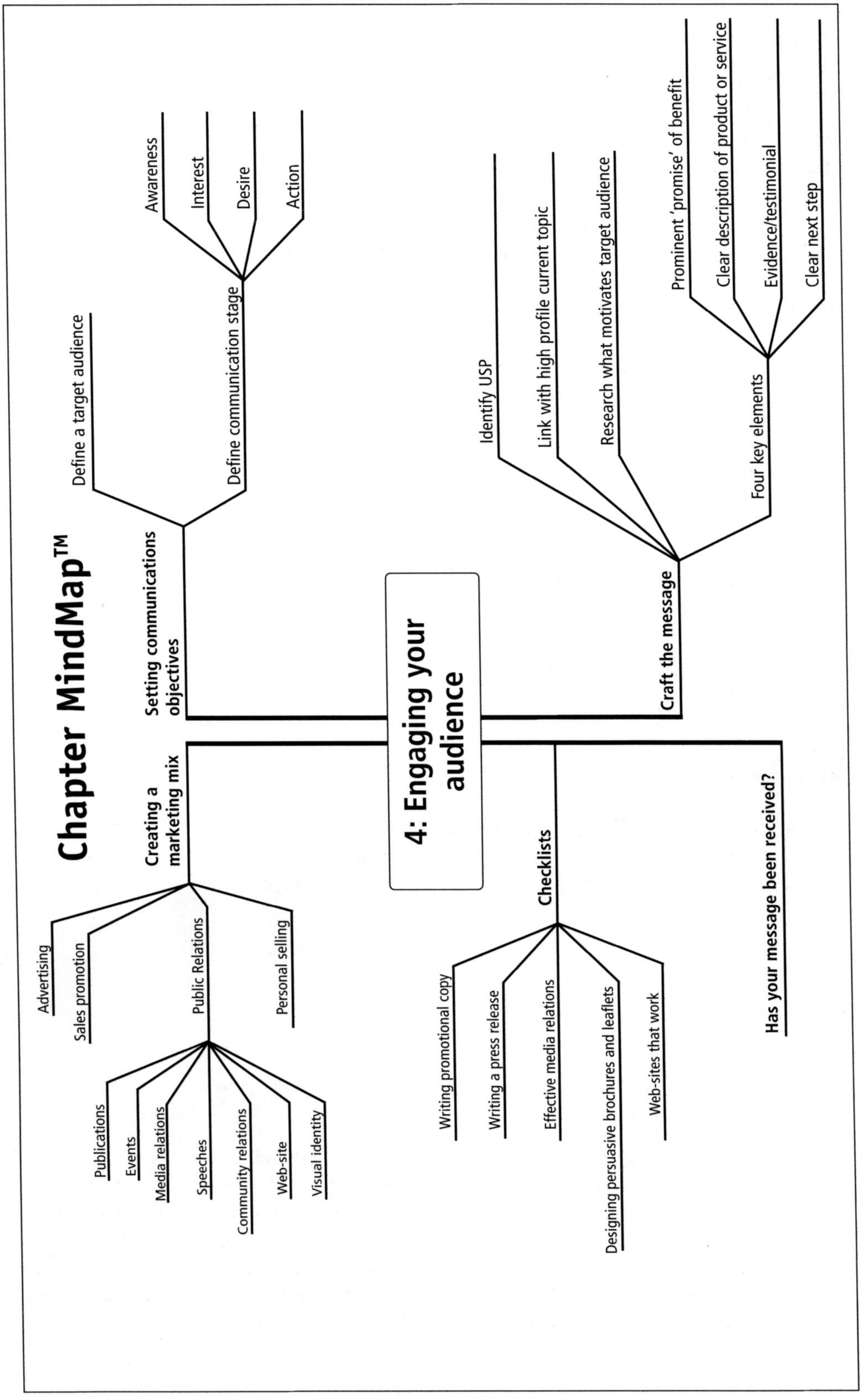
Chapter MindMap™
4: Engaging your audience
Setting communications objectives
Define a target audience
Define communication stage
Awareness
Interest
Desire
Action
Craft the message
Identify USP
Link with high profile current topic
Research what motivates target audience
Four key elements
Prominent 'promise' of benefit
Clear description of product or service
Evidence/testimonial
Clear next step
Creating a marketing mix
Advertising
Sales promotion
Public Relations
Personal selling
Publications
Events
Media relations
Speeches
Community relations
Web-site
Visual identity
Checklists
Writing promotional copy
Writing a press release
Effective media relations
Designing persuasive brochures and leaflets
Web-sites that work
Has your message been received?

5 Working in partnership

Developing successful partnership initiatives with external agencies, other sectors and customers can create learning communities which are robust and able to improve continuously their performance.

The Work Foundation, Managing Best Practice 33

Seeing the bigger picture

It can be easy, particularly when focusing on the detail of your own organisation, to lose sight of the bigger picture. Perhaps the most effective way of avoiding this is to work with other organisations to form partnerships.

Establishing a network is part of the basic survival process for any individual, group or organisation these days. It often used to be possible to receive all your funding and to meet all your targets largely on your own. However, the necessity, and even the requirement, to work with others to deliver common objectives is becoming the norm. Increasingly, adequate funding, even for core activities, must be contracted or bid for by a group of partners. In addition to that basic survival requirement, learning providers, in particular, need allies and partners to help them to reach people's lives.

Partnerships seem to be favoured by government and other important funders as a means of distributing resources and ensuring regional and local collaboration, consultation and feedback. A number of models of partnership have been introduced, which set out the types of organisations that government expects to take part.

It is clear, therefore, that working in partnership makes it easier to plan activities within the context of wider political, environmental, social and community developments, as well as allowing learning providers and others to tap into a greater variety of resources and funding streams. What is not so widely

recognised is the value of like-minded organisations grouping together to 'warm up' the potential audience to learning services in general as a 'one-off' umbrella marketing campaign or as a reflection of national initiatives like Adult Learners' Week, Family Learning Week, Learning at Work Day or National Bike Week. A local radio station or newspaper is more likely to make a big feature of local learning provision, whether it's tasters, fun events or regular courses, when it can give out information about a wide choice of learning opportunities over the whole of the area covered by that station or publication (see Chapter 4).

The purpose of marketing learning is, after all, to expand the market for everyone, rather than to intensify competition between learning providers. It is in the interest of everyone involved in providing learning opportunities that a culture is developed that significantly enlarges the existing constituency of lifelong learners.

The pros and cons of working with others

At a Lifelong Learning Conference run by Hampshire County Council a few years ago, delegates from a wide range of sectors were asked what were the possible reasons for working in partnership and what might be the possible drawbacks. Their answers reflect the fears and expectations of many groups when they contemplate forming a partnership, and are worth repeating:

Reasons for working with partners can be to:

- share values and perceptions;
- help shape strategy and direction;
- respond to specific initiatives;
- gain knowledge and share information;
- form partnerships across different interest groups;
- help participants to do their own jobs more effectively;
- assist the democratic process/local consultation;

case study

Case study: London Voices, London Choices

A steering group representing learning providers and campaigners formed a partnership to promote Adult Learners' Week across London. Their objective was to encourage more providers to put on courses and tasters during the week and to help them promote those courses to potential learners as widely as possible. Common themes were devised in successive years (London Voices and London Choices) as an umbrella promotional idea to attract more press coverage. With such a broad-ranging concept for a theme, tasters from fitness training to holiday Spanish could all be promoted together. The opportunity to publicise leisure activities alongside more formal subjects also proved a winning formula for enticing people to try new things. The joint effort allowed a very small amount of money to go a long way. Partners included: Sport England, London's Museums Archives and Libraries, a London Learning Partnership, individual London Further Education colleges, NIACE, Campaign for Learning, Government Office for London, Workers' Educational Association, BBC, National Literacy Trust, Department for Culture, Media and Sport, Adult Basic Skills Strategy Unit, Floodlight, Arts Council – London, Further Education London Region Services and a representative from the marketing group of London's five Learning and Skills Councils.

- identify real local learning needs;
- attract funding/maximise resources;
- convey a vision;
- benefit from new ideas/innovative thinking;
- challenge preconceptions;
- initiate local projects;
- provide more informal/less threatening local contact point;
- involve potential learners.

Possible drawbacks can be that:

- you may stimulate demand that is inadequately resourced;
- there is a danger of becoming a 'talking shop';
- administration and organisation is difficult;
- there is a lack of accountability;
- the management structure is weak;
- a lack of 'joined-up government' can make it difficult to work across local authority departments where necessary;
- there is a danger of being dominated by personalities/sectors;
- partnerships mean more meetings which involve more travel;
- there is often uncertainty about payment for attendance at meetings;
- there are problems in mixing statutory government bodies with informal groups;
- there is uncertainty about democratic accountability;
- some client groups are under-represented and therefore lack opportunity for input;
- priorities often reflect those of the 'lead' organisation.

What is clearly necessary is for partners to set out with a vision of what they want to achieve and a realistic idea of how to manage the initiative so as to avoid some of the pitfalls.

Making partnerships work

Local Authorities make useful and sometimes essential partners and very often initiate partnerships themselves. The Local Government National Training Organisation (LGNTO) is therefore well placed to give good advice about how to review particular partnerships with a view to making them work better. The figure below is based on their suggested model for partnerships that work.

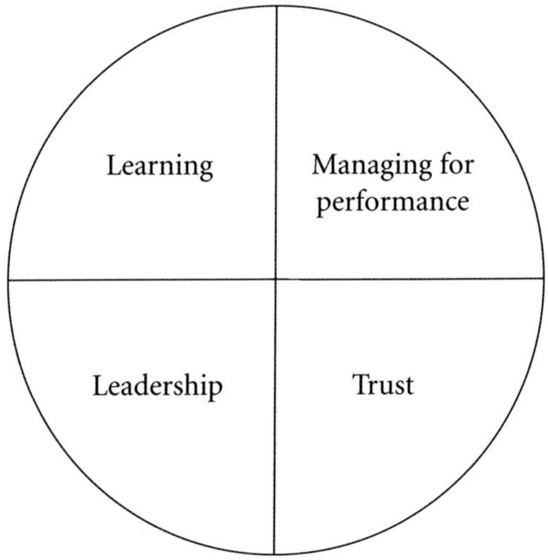

Leadership

Leadership is a tricky word. Judging by some of the fears expressed above, there is a fine balance to be struck between a dominating 'lead' organisation or personality and a partnership lapsing into a weak structure where nothing gets done. Where there is successful leadership, the whole really is greater than the sum of the parts, and partners who share identified aims, objectives and vision have a better chance of delivering them.

This does not rule out a 'lead' partner or facilitator. At least at the beginning, someone will need to get the group together. That person or organisation should, however, quickly move to a position of sharing the role by encouraging the group to adopt a broad management structure from the outset.

Adopting a neutral meeting ground; alternating the chair at meetings; encouraging the early establishment of common aims and objectives; giving a name to the partnership; identifying the particular skills and attributes that each partner can bring to the group and assigning tasks and roles; addressing the 'what's in it for us?' and 'what am I doing here?' questions; making sure that communications and administration systems are set up; these are all policies that will encourage partners to pull together and make a real effort to achieve shared goals.

Trust

It is important that partners have an equal say in decision-making and are mutually accountable for their contributions. A balance of risks and rewards to partners should be constantly addressed so that everyone understands how easy or difficult it is for each partner to contribute in the context of the rest of their life/job/employer's business objectives. Sometimes individuals who are sent to represent an organisation do not see the task as being as important as other more mainstream parts of their job, and sometimes they have little support from their line manager.

Where there is frustration or conflict among partners, it needs to be addressed promptly and mutual expectations and required standards clarified in the context of the immediate problem. For example, if a partner does not attend meetings, respond to communications or carry out assigned tasks, it may be necessary to find out if their failure to contribute is due to personal reasons, pressure of work, or lack of enthusiasm from their employer organisation. Support can then be offered or relations established with an alternative representative of that organisation.

Strategies for avoiding people dropping out or failing to pull their weight can include: helping other partners achieve their own objectives through the partnership; making sure that information about progress and benefits are passed on to partner organisations directly, not just via the representative who attends; seeking win-win solutions that clearly give partners the benefits they seek; helping less-well-resourced partners build their confidence and 'have their say'; and reviewing the effectiveness of current communications.

Exclusive, judgemental and status-conscious attitudes do not help mutual trust, nor does a blame culture. Encouraging a 'can do' approach to objectives, looking for ways in which each partner can make a valued contribution, and creating opportunities for people to get to know each other as individuals, will go a long way towards building the trust that partners need to keep the partnership together and realise a shared vision.

Learning

Learning is arguably the most important aspect of a successful partnership, because a joint venture needs to have an 'organic' rather a rigid structure. In order to take account of unforeseen influences and to make best use of all their talents and resources, partners need continuously to learn from each other and from outside experience.

Using a resource such as this one; looking at how others have managed similar projects; planning regular evaluation and feedback; piloting new ideas and learning from the results; mentoring, shadowing and informally learning from other partners, can all maximise everyone's learning opportunities and enhance individual skills and overall understanding of the project.

It can be very helpful to ask each partner on a regular basis the question, "What did you learn through the partnership (this month) that helped: your personal development; your career; your organisation's objectives; the aims of the partnership?" While identifying what each participant can offer the partnership at the beginning is important, periodic reviews, even if quite informal, can help to indicate how the group is coming together (or not!) and what has been achieved to date.

Opportunities to learn together and to report on learning experiences (especially in a social or informal setting) will make people aware of each other's strengths and interests. When questioned, most people will say that they learn a lot from their mistakes. Identifying what has not gone so well, both for individuals and the group, can not only be a great ice-breaker and leveller but will lead to more realistic forward planning.

Managing for performance

All the hopes, fears and objectives of a partnership can count for nothing if leadership, trust and learning do not lead to tangible outcomes. To help the partnership manage change, celebrate what is being achieved, build on strengths and deliver objectives, partner roles, responsibilities and outcomes need to be identified and assigned.

Shared ownership of the vision is key, but practical objectives, targets and milestones also need to be owned by all partners, with each knowing exactly what they are expected to do to deliver the next part of the plan. All partners should be involved in devising the strategic plan and should agree to their part in its delivery. It will not be possible to please everybody all of the time and some partners may have to learn new ways of working.

If the primary purpose, or an important part of the partnership, is to promote learning, say, under a national campaign, problems can occur in mixing marketing professionals with other staff. Most FE colleges and government-funded bodies will have a marketing department and the person who represents them on promotional matters will have some training in marketing. However, other partners may send people from a variety of employment backgrounds. In these circumstances, it is even more important to have a clear strategy based on similar principles to those set out in other parts of this book.

Marketing is an area of expertise that everyone thinks they know about. Some people will come to the table with a preconceived idea of what advertising media to use, e.g. 'just like the leaflet we did last year'. The fact that it was sent out too late, was completely untargeted (one size fits all); with mixed messages and bad graphics, and that 20,000 of them ended up in boxes under someone's desk, can sometimes be forgotten in the enthusiasm to 'tick the box'. Chapter 6 explains the importance of learning from your own and others' marketing mistakes.

Who makes a good partner?

The variety of organisations which might have an interest in promoting learning is huge. Checklist 8 sets out 'usual' and 'not-so-usual' possible partners, indicating a range of environments where learning could take place, or information about learning activities might be displayed or made available. Thinking about where your target audience goes every day can concentrate the mind on a realistic approach to marketing learning.

Posters and leaflets in the local fish and chip shop, gym, leisure centre, pub or hairdresser are a start, but what about including the chip shop owners in your partnership? That might involve a quiz about marine life that starts in the fish shop but ends in the library or college. You would be making the learning connections, promoting learning courses and activities and helping to break down some of the barriers mentioned in Chapter 1. Creating alliances with groups or organisations not traditionally thought of as contributing to learning can be one of the most effective ways of reaching out into the community.

Choice of partners also depends on what you want to deliver and which other organisations could benefit from being involved. There is no harm in setting up a preliminary meeting to see what different people can bring to the table and only proceeding with those who are really suitable. There is rarely (except with a few very rigid funding streams) a rule that says you can't drop partners from the group if it doesn't work out with them, or one that stops the partnership from expanding to include other useful partners at a later date.

LGNTO's useful checklist has eight tests, which are set out below. They are aimed at answering the question 'How healthy and effective is your partnership?' Partners who share and demonstrate these priorities are likely to be successful.

- Partners can demonstrate **real results through collaboration.**
- **Common interest** supersedes partners' interest.
- Partners **use "we"** when talking about partner matters.
- Partners are **mutually accountable** for tasks and outcomes.
- Partners **share** responsibilities and rewards.
- Partners strive to develop and maintain **trust**.
- Partners are **willing to change** what they do and how they do it.
- Partners **seek to improve** how the partnership performs.

Encouraging learner input

There is an increasing awareness of the importance of putting people before structures in providing learning. In the Further Education sector, for example, colleges are already expected to consult employers and the community when preparing funding bids.

It is an extension of this process to regard the relationship with the learner as a partnership. This can often mean encouraging learner input into course design and even creating bespoke courses.

Experience has proved that involving the learner in designing the curriculum can be

case study

East Durham Community College

At East Durham Community College a team of eight community development officers liaise with community groups to establish local needs and develop a relevant curriculum. A committee of town and parish councillors advises the college on what is appropriate to their area. Each community has its own prospectus and enrolment, and delivery of learning takes place in village halls, community centres and youth clubs.

one of the most effective guarantees of course success. This is hardly surprising since the learner has 'bought into' the relationship from the very beginning. This form of relationship marketing is frequently taken for granted elsewhere. Customer loyalty schemes, discussed in Chapter 3, are built upon the same principles.

Many organisations involved in producing goods and services have also realised the importance of the existing customer in recruitment. Anyone who is a member of a book or music club will be familiar with the scheme whereby rewards are offered for recruiting a friend. The same process can work effectively in promoting learning opportunities. Indeed, some adult education institutions employ exactly the same technique, offering discounts on enrolment to those who actively recruit new learners.

The most powerful advertisement for the learning opportunities that you provide will be those learners who have already benefited from them. In marketing terms the learner is a key player and the relationship between him or her and the provider is critical. If a real partnership is established, both stand to benefit.

Marketing the partnership

It is worth remembering that the mere fact that a partnership has been set up is newsworthy in itself. It may be interesting to readers, listeners and viewers of the local media to know that people are working together to cater for their needs.

Press releases that flag up how partners are working together for the benefit of the local community can have added impact.

It is important that your own staff are aware that the partnership exists, so make sure you let staff know before you release any external communications.

Research suggests that learners can be confused by the plethora of learning messages and brands with which they are often bombarded. Partnerships can help clarify the message and present a more united and simple point of contact for the learner.

case study

Press release: 'Totton College signs new community partnership deal'

The new partnership project (Youth and Families Matter) will make a real difference to families in Totton and the surrounding area...

... YFM Project manager, Roger Frapwell, explains "Many of the people referred to us are those in most need of support and guidance. Some might be those who are 'victims' of our society, others have suffered as a result of family breakdown or are struggling owing to low confidence. Helping such people has been at the heart of 'Youth and Families Matter' since the project started ten years ago, but resources are naturally restricted, which is why the Partnership with Totton College is so exciting. Partnership has always been key for us, as we believe we can achieve more together than apart."

Potential Local Partners — Checklist 8

- ✓ Pre-school groups
- ✓ Nurseries
- ✓ Schools
- ✓ Colleges
- ✓ Universities
- ✓ Adult learners' centres
- ✓ Libraries
- ✓ Hospitals
- ✓ Churches
- ✓ Surgeries
- ✓ Old people's homes
- ✓ Homeless shelters
- ✓ Shopping centres
- ✓ Prisons
- ✓ Football clubs
- ✓ Bookshops
- ✓ Museums
- ✓ Galleries
- ✓ Parks
- ✓ Restaurants
- ✓ Post Offices
- ✓ Careers services
- ✓ Citizen's Advice Bureaux
- ✓ Local charities and campaigning groups

Typical Local Partnerships — Checklist 9

- ✓ Lifelong learning partnerships
- ✓ Early years development partnerships
- ✓ Rural partnerships
- ✓ Environment and sustainability partnerships
- ✓ Connexions partnerships
- ✓ Regeneration partnerships
- ✓ Community safety partnerships
- ✓ Public health partnerships
- ✓ E-government partnerships

Chapter Summary

Partnerships have many benefits and are often required for funding bids. Making partnerships work relies on a combination of leadership, trust, learning and managing for performance. A healthy partnership will exhibit eight key factors. Successful partnerships should be publicised both internally and externally.

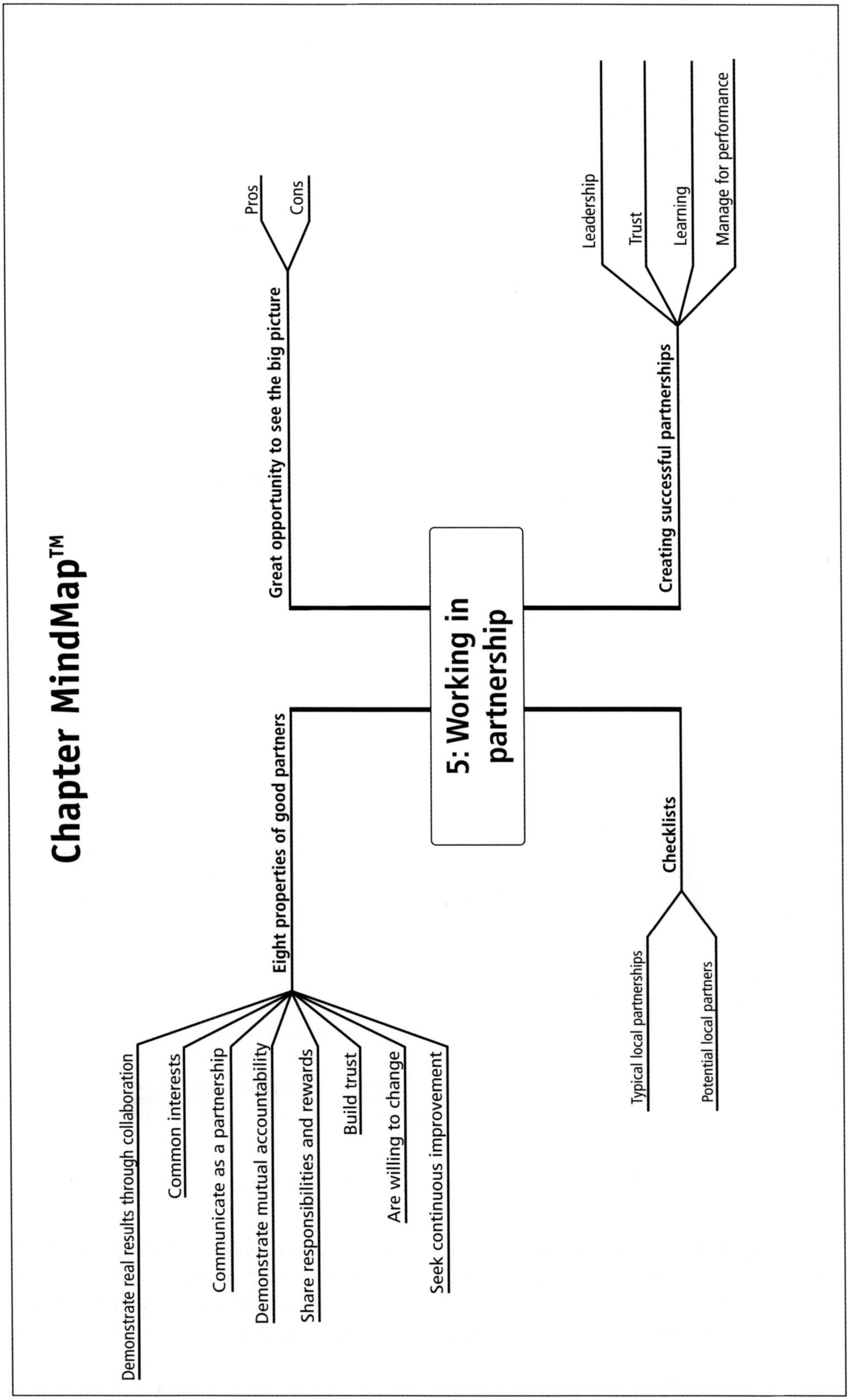
Chapter MindMap™
5: Working in partnership
Eight properties of good partners
Demonstrate real results through collaboration
Common interests
Communicate as a partnership
Demonstrate mutual accountability
Share responsibilities and rewards
Build trust
Are willing to change
Seek continuous improvement
Great opportunity to see the big picture
Pros
Cons
Creating successful partnerships
Leadership
Trust
Learning
Manage for performance
Checklists
Typical local partnerships
Potential local partners

6 Evaluation

Checking against the plan

The success of any marketing activity is defined by how well it has met the objectives originally defined in the marketing plan. If the objectives have been clearly defined in the initial planning, the process of evaluation should be relatively straightforward. The controls section of the plan will detail how progress against the plan will be monitored and how corrective action will be taken. It is important that evaluation is an ongoing process so that slippage against targets can be identified early and corrective action taken. Annual reviews will tell you whether or not you have achieved targets but give you no opportunity to get back on track.

Performance monitoring

The five 'Ps' of marketing (product, price, place, promotion, people) can all be monitored to build up a picture of how well the marketing plan is progressing. Targets for each 'P' should be defined in the marketing plan. It is likely that there will be several targets that relate to both individual classes as well as overall factors such as the learning environment and enquiry handling. Examples are given in Table 8.

'P'	Example targets	Monitoring technique
Product (or service)	• Achieve 80% enrolment on all badminton classes between January and June. • Achieve 90% repeat bookings for baby massage classes over 12 months. • Achieve 90% customer satisfaction for telephone enquiry handling on all calls over a three-month period.	• Keep records of enrolment and review regularly against target. • Implement and review regular customer-satisfaction surveys. • Keep customer database that tracks all contacts with customers so 'loyalty' can be monitored and rate of attracting new customers measured.
Price	• Break even on new family computing club with a price of £1 per family per visit during the first three months of operation.	• Keep records of attendance, income and expenditure.

Place	• Achieve annual improvement of customer satisfaction with learning environment of 5% over the year.	• Implement and review customer-satisfaction survey.
Promotion	• Achieve communications objectives defined in communications strategy.	• Survey local residents to establish awareness levels of the venue or specific classes. • Monitor costs of promotion against number of people reached, number of enquiries generated and number of enrolments achieved.
People	• Achieve 95% complaint-handling satisfaction rating over the year. • Achieve 90% employee-satisfaction rating over the year. • Achieve Investor in People status by the end of the year.	• Include complaint-handling assessment in regular customer-satisfaction surveys • Develop and implement employee- satisfaction survey. • Pursue Investor in People accreditation.

Table 8

Monitoring and measurement tools and techniques

The combination of just four key tools should tell you how well your marketing plan is performing overall. The tools are described in Table 9.

Customer-satisfaction survey

Organisations that achieve high customer-satisfaction levels audit their service performance on a regular, ongoing basis. They conduct research to establish what customers regard as important components of good service and then monitor their performance levels for each component.

Defining excellent service

Don't assume that you and your colleagues already know what your customers or service users would define as good service. Develop a framework through discussion and then road-test it by consulting with both users and non-users. Suggestions for questions that will help you define excellent service are given below.

- Describe an occasion when you experienced excellent service at our venue. What particularly made the experience so satisfactory? What would you suggest we do to make that level of service an everyday experience?
- Please rank the list of performance indicators given here to indicate which are the most and least important to you. (Present respondent with list of factors that you and your colleagues have generated.)

	Information captured	Frequency	Delivery method
Customer-satisfaction survey	Customer feedback on specific classes/activities/sessions and overall quality of the venue. Information to identify progress against targets.	Quarterly to six-monthly	Evaluation forms from classes/activities/sessions and access to forms in reception area for customers who are not attending organised activities. Encourage customers to complete forms with prize draw.
Customer-relationship management (CRM) database reports	Quantitative information about customers and response to promotion campaigns.	Monthly	All service use and enquiry responses to be captured and entered onto database.
Community survey	Feedback from the wider community, including non-users, on how well venue is meeting community needs and potential for improvement. Also evaluation of local media coverage.	Six-monthly	Questionnaire distributed to community, consultation with community leaders and other market-research techniques described in Chapter 2.
Employee-satisfaction survey	Feedback from employees into their ability to meet customer needs.	Six-monthly	Questionnaire distributed to staff – either hard copy or on-line.

Table 9

➲ Describe an occasion when you were particularly unhappy with our service. What factors led to your dissatisfaction? How do you think we could avoid similar experiences in the future?

Complaints (or lack of) are a good indicator of customer satisfaction. On average, a customer tells three people about a good experience, but a dissatisfied customer will tell about eleven people. Customers whose complaints are satisfactorily resolved often become more satisfied than customers who never complained at all. Analyse the complaints that have been recorded over the last few months to establish performance criteria that can then become part of your customer-satisfaction survey.

Include questions about the respondent in your survey so that you can analyse how well you are doing with specific target audiences. You may find that some target audiences are more satisfied than others.

As a result of your consultation and analysis you will be able to develop a customer-satisfaction survey that is tailored to your particular circumstances. A checklist that describes the types of criteria that are often included in customer-satisfaction surveys is given at the end of this chapter.

Delivery of the customer-satisfaction survey

You will want to capture customer feedback on individual classes and activities as well as the overall centre environment and service. Guaranteeing anonymity is important to ensure honest responses, so although you may choose to distribute the surveys in class they should be returned to a central, accessible collection point. Many venues survey customers once a year but a fuller picture will be built through more regular surveys, perhaps once a quarter. Combining the evaluation of both classes and the entire centre in one form will streamline the evaluation process. It will also provide an overview of how satisfaction varies throughout the year and according to the service used.

Criteria	**A: Customer importance (ranked out of 10)**	**B: Customer satisfaction (ranked out of 10)**	**C: Total satisfaction value (A x B)**
Centre cleanliness	9	5	45
Centre opening times	9	7	63
Staff ability to resolve problems	6	8	48
Car parking	9	5	45
Public transport	5	2	10
Total satisfaction value (sum of all items in C)			211
Customer Satisfaction Index(expressed as a percentage (sum of column C/max possible value x 100)			211/500 x 100= 42%

Calculating a Customer Satisfaction Index™
It is possible to produce a quantitative, numerical value for customer satisfaction by combining importance ratings and satisfaction ratings to give an overall score. The advantage of this approach is that a single number can be used to represent customer satisfaction. The number can be used for comparison over a period of time even if the questions asked in the survey change. This gives you the opportunity to consistently track your performance over time, whilst at the same time evaluating different criteria as your customers' needs change. A simple example is given below. In this example the five factors listed were identified as the five most important to customers in the consultation carried out before the customer-satisfaction survey implementation.

The process to calculate the Customer Satisfaction Index™ will be the same even if the top five most important factors change, providing a consistent measure of satisfaction over time. The aim of this approach is to 'do best at what matters most to customers'.

Customer-relationship management database

No matter what market you are in, it is less effort to retain an existing customer than to attract a new one. Many successful commercial companies work on developing a strong customer relationship, known as 'customer relationship management' or CRM, to make the most of their existing customer base.

A key CRM tool is a customer database that records all interactions with the customer as well as their individual details. The individual details can be used to contact the customer and to track which sectors of the community are using your services. Details kept on the database can include:

- Title
- First and last name
- Gender
- Age
- Ethnicity
- Disability
- Full address
- E-mail address
- Employment status
- Marital status
- Number of children
- Car owner
- Courses/classes/sessions attended
- Courses/classes/sessions enquired about
- Promotion that stimulated enquiry

Every customer contact should be used as an opportunity to capture more details. The first time someone contacts your venue by telephone it will probably only be practical to capture name and address details and their areas of interest. Further details can be captured if they attend a class so that a full profile is built up over a period of time.

The CRM database is an ideal tool for recording the level of response gained from different promotions. It is at the point of first contact that the customer is most likely to remember what stimulated their enquiry. By the time they physically start attending a class they will probably have forgotten the initial trigger. Any enquiry about your centre's services is an opportunity to create a new customer record. This will not only enable you to monitor response to publicity but also to create a list of people who can then be targeted with more information about their areas of interest.

Monthly reports from your CRM database will provide much of the information you need to monitor the success of your marketing plan. Simplified example reports are given below.

The enquiry analysis will show which promotion methods are working best. Word of mouth will normally be the most cited source of information but don't conclude that this means other forms of promotion are not useful. 'Word of mouth' is a complex category that covers a multitude of sources and relies on

Enquiry analysis May 2003 XYZ Leisure Centre

	Subject of enquiry			
Source of enquiry	**General**	**Football**	**Swimming**	**Computer Club**
Word of mouth	240	23	76	12
Bus adverts	45	12	9	3
Town centre leaflet distribution	204	56	78	23
Reference in local media	20	5	12	0
Mailing	45	32	45	67

Attendance analysis May 2003 XYZ Leisure Centre

	Class / activity / session				
Customer details	**Swimming**	**Football**	**Pilates**	**Family Computer Club**	**Baby massage**
Total numbers	500	230	40	60	60
Male	150	200	4	20	10
Female	350	30	36	40	20
0 – 10 years	150	0	0	20	30

Customer details	Class / activity / session				
	Swimming	**Football**	**Pilates**	**Family Computer Club**	**Baby massage**
11 – 18 years	50	150	0	10	0
19 – 26 years	100	50	10	10	15
27 – 40 years	100	30	0	10	15
40 – 55 years	100	0	10	5	0
Over 55 years	0	0	0	5	0
Post code area 1	400	150	30	40	45
Post code area 2	50	50	5	10	10
Post code area 3	50	30	5	10	5

a baseline level of communication to keep it stimulated. If you removed the formal communications channels of advertising, public relations and mailings, the 'word of mouth' would become less effective.

The attendance analysis will tell you what progress you are making against the targets in your marketing plan. The enquiry analysis will tell you if you are achieving your communication objectives.

Community survey

The CRM database will tell you whether you have been successful in attracting your target audiences into the centre. Your customer-satisfaction survey will capture customer feedback on the quality of their experience. However, neither of these tools will tell you why non-users have not yet visited your venue.

Understanding the needs of people who are still not using your services will require further, ongoing market research in the community. Your original research, as described in Chapter 2, should be repeated at regular intervals, with modifications, to explore how the community's perception of your services is changing. Your communications objectives will help you modify the research to reflect the development of your marketing plan. For example, if you are promoting a new crèche as

case study

Evaluating learning through football

Playing for Success (PfS) was established in 1997 by the Department for Education and Skills (DfES) in partnership with the Football Association (FA) Premier League, the Nationwide League and Local Education Authorities (LEAs). It set up out-of-school-hours study-support centres within top football clubs and other sports clubs. The centres use football and other sports to help motivate pupils, identified by their schools, as being in need of assistance to help them get back up to speed in literacy, numeracy and information and communication technology (ICT).

Evaluation

The National Foundation for Educational Research (NFER) has carried out four national evaluations of the programme. The first looked at the first six centres to open and found significant gains amongst pupils attending. The second, covering 12 centres, found gains of even greater significance. The third evaluation, of 27 centres, showed even more significant gains. The report of the fourth survey found that:

- on average primary pupils improved their numeracy scores by an average of 17 months, and secondary pupils by 24 months;
- whilst primary pupils' reading comprehension did not quite reach statistical significance, secondary pupils' performance improved by 8 months;
- pupils' ICT skills improved significantly;
- pupils made significant progress in their independent study skills and self-image, and parents and teachers noticed particular improvements in their attitudes to education; PfS reached its target group of underachieving pupils with improvements regardless of gender, deprivation, ethnicity or fluency in English.

one of the key strengths of your venue, the research will need to test that the community is aware of its existence.

Media evaluation

The enquiry analysis from your CRM database will tell you how many enquiries are generated from media coverage, but you should also keep a record of coverage in print and broadcast media as it appears – regardless of whether enquiries are generated. The media evaluation can be part of your community survey as it reflects the image of your venue as it appears in the local media. You could use a clippings agency to capture coverage as it occurs but it will be cheaper to make sure one of your own staff scans the local papers on a weekly basis. It is more difficult to monitor radio coverage, unless the station is responding to one of your own releases, in which case you can simply ask when they will be using your news. If something about your venue appears on local radio it is likely that someone among your network of friends, family and colleagues will hear it, so encourage them to pass on to you any details for your records.

There are a number of methods that can be used to evaluate the impact of media coverage. The simplest is just to record the number of pieces that appear. The circulation of the publication is also often used as a measurement method. While it can seem impressive for an article to appear in a newspaper with a circulation of 50,000 people, it is worth considering how many of these people are within reach of your venue. Two articles in a publication that has a circulation of only 8,000 but is available entirely within convenient travelling distance of your venue will have a greater impact on your attendances.

Stakeholder survey

There will be a group of people in your community whose opinion of your venue is important even though they may not be regular, or likely to be future, customers. They are the people who may influence the success of developments such as funding proposals, planning applications and other community issues. They include local councillors as well as senior council officials, leaders of local associations, opinion formers in local media, major suppliers and large employers.

Make sure you know who these people are and what they think about your venue. Canvass their opinions regularly through networking events in the community. These are busy people who may not have the time to return surveys but they should be few enough in number for you to establish personal relationships with a core group.

	Males		**Females**		**All of population**
	Full-time	**Part-time**	**Full-time**	**Part-time**	
Very satisfied	7	10	7	9	7
Satisfied	42	50	49	54	47
Neither satisfied nor dissatisfied	28	26	28	25	27
Dissatisfied	20	12	14	10	16
Very dissatisfied	4	1	2	2	3

Table 10: Workplace Employee Relations Survey, Department of Trade and Industry, 1998

Employee-satisfaction survey

Excellently managed service companies believe that employee satisfaction has a direct impact on customer satisfaction. A regular employee-satisfaction survey will help you identify issues that could affect customer satisfaction before they become serious. You can also use any regular staff consultative meetings to spot problems. Job satisfaction tends to vary by gender and method of working. Table 10 shows national job-satisfaction levels as reported in a 1998 survey by gender and full- or part-time working.

A checklist of factors to include in the survey is given at the end of the chapter. The checklist includes whether staff would recommend their workplace to others. An NOP survey carried out in 2000 found that on average 73% of employees would recommend their place of work to a friend. In 2003 a survey carried out for Learning at Work Day found that this figure rose to 87% if the workplace had a supportive learning culture. You should road-test the checklist with a selection of staff before it is widely distributed to make sure these factors are important to your employees. By including an importance and satisfaction

Criteria	A: Employee importance (ranked out of 10)	B: Employee satisfaction (ranked out of 10)	C: Total satisfaction value (A x B)
Opportunities to learn and develop	9	6	54
Information to help customers	9	4	36
Department/team Co-operation	6	5	30
Feedback on job performance	7	6	42
Believe venue is meeting community needs	8	8	64
Total satisfaction value (sum of all items in C)			226
Employee Satisfaction Index‰ expressed as a percentage (sum of column C/max possible value x 100)			226/500 x 100 = 45%

Table 11: Employee-satisfaction Index

rating in your survey you can work towards 'doing best at what matters to employees most'.

Investors in People

The Investors in People standard is a tried-and-tested flexible framework that helps organisations succeed and compete through improved people performance. Research among 2000 organisations who have Investors in People status found that 80% had increased customer satisfaction levels once they were accredited.

Employee-satisfaction index

By asking staff for an importance and satisfaction rating you can determine an employee-satisfaction index in a similar fashion to the Customer Satisfaction Index™. A simplified, worked example is given in Table 11, on page 75.

The employee-satisfaction index will provide a more in-depth analysis of satisfaction than simply asking employees to indicate how satisfied they are on a scale that ranges from very dissatisfied to very satisfied. Questions should also be asked to capture details of job type, department and level to establish any trends that arise in individual teams or job types.

Customer-satisfaction Surveys Checklist 10

Typical areas to explore include:

Questions relating to the venue

- ✓ cleanliness
- ✓ equipment availability
- ✓ equipment condition
- ✓ cancellation procedures for classes or activities
- ✓ information and advice given by staff
- ✓ staff ability to resolve problems
- ✓ ease of contacting venue by telephone
- ✓ value for money of activities/classes
- ✓ opening times
- ✓ public transport access
- ✓ car parking

Questions relating to the respondent

- ✓ gender
- ✓ age
- ✓ ethnicity
- ✓ disability
- ✓ area of residence
- ✓ employment status
- ✓ frequency of respondent's visits to the venue
- ✓ mode of transport to venue

Questions relating to class/activity/session

- ✓ extent to which teacher/leader met individual's needs
- ✓ punctuality of teacher/leader
- ✓ expertise/competence of teacher/leader
- ✓ opportunities to ask questions
- ✓ opportunities for identifying progression routes to learn more
- ✓ condition of class/activity environment and equipment
- ✓ likelihood of recommending the class to others

Employee-satisfaction Surveys Checklist 11

Typical areas to explore include:

- ✓ opportunities to learn and develop
- ✓ co-operation between departments/teams
- ✓ clear understanding of roles and responsibilities
- ✓ clear, regular feedback on job performance
- ✓ good, regular information about organisational aims and objectives
- ✓ good, regular information about departmental aims and objectives
- ✓ information available to satisfy customer enquiries
- ✓ systems/processes/resources available to satisfy customer needs
- ✓ whether they would recommend employer to a friend
- ✓ how far venue is meeting community needs
- ✓ how far good service quality is provided to customers

Chapter Summary

Evaluation is based on how well the targets defined in the marketing plan are being met. Four measurement tools can be used to supply the necessary information: customer-satisfaction survey; customer-relationship management database; community; survey and employee- satisfaction survey.

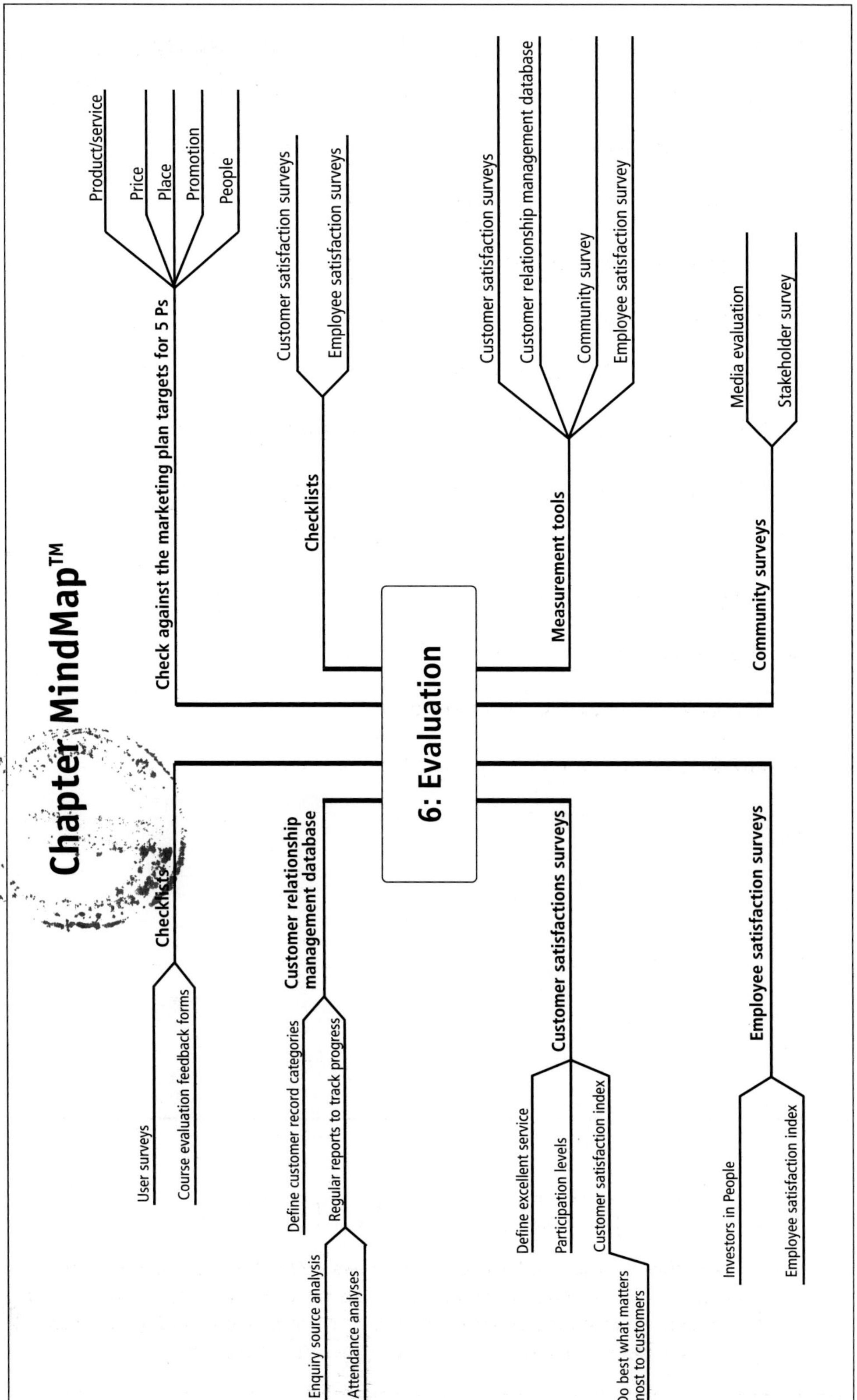
Chapter MindMap™
6: Evaluation
Check against the marketing plan targets for 5 Ps
Product/service
Price
Place
Promotion
People
Checklists
Customer satisfaction surveys
Employee satisfaction surveys
Measurement tools
Customer satisfaction surveys
Customer relationship management database
Community survey
Employee satisfaction survey
Community surveys
Media evaluation
Stakeholder survey
Checklists
User surveys
Course evaluation feedback forms
Customer relationship management database
Define customer record categories
Regular reports to track progress
Enquiry source analysis
Attendance analyses
Customer satisfactions surveys
Define excellent service
Participation levels
Customer satisfaction index
Do best what matters most to customers
Employee satisfaction surveys
Investors in People
Employee satisfaction index

Resources

Additional resources to those found throughout this book, are listed below.

Marketing resources

Marketing Management: International Edition by Philip Kotler, US Imports & PHIPEs
A classic book on marketing, updated to include technological developments.

Principles of Marketing: European Edition by Philip Kotler et al, FT Prentice Hall
A comprehensive introduction to modern marketing.

The Chartered Institute of Marketing
The Chartered Institute of Marketing is the global professional body for marketing which develops professional standards and practice. www.cim.co.uk

Key Note
Produces market reports on consumer goods and industries, and market assessment reports on lifestyles sectors. www.keynote.co.uk

Mintel
UK market research database, producing reports on themes including leisure. www.mintel.co.uk

Useful sources of funding and support

Awards for All
A Lottery grants programme aimed at local communities with grants between £500 and £5000. www.awardsforall.org.uk

Big Lottery Fund
Formerly the New Opportunities Fund and the Community Fund. It will award grants to education, health and environment projects, and support charities and voluntary groups in greatest need. For more information visit: www.culture.gov.uk

Department for Culture, Media and Sport
Department responsible for Government policy on sport, recreation and leisure. www.culture.gov.uk

Department for Education and Skills
Details of Government initiatives and funding opportunities can be found at www.dfes.gov.uk

The Football Foundation
The UK's largest sports charity with a £53m per year investment into the grass roots of football. www.footballfoundation.org.uk

Foundation for Sports and the Arts
Uses income from the football pools promoters to give grants to a wide range of projects. Tel: 0151 259 5505.

Inclusive Fitness Initiative
Supports opportunities for people with disabilities to take part in physical activities.
www.inclusivefitness.org

Sports Councils
England/Scotland/Northern Ireland/Wales
Work to promote participation in sports.
www.sportengland.org
www.sportscotland.org.uk
www.sportni.net
www.sports-council-wales.co.uk

Sportsmatch
A grassroots sponsorship incentive scheme which matches commercial sponsorship.
www.sportsmatch.co.uk

The National Lottery
Funds six good causes – arts, sports, charities, heritage, millennium projects and education, health and environment.
www.national-lottery.co.uk

NIACE
NIACE aims to advance the interest of adult learners and potential learners in England and Wales.
www.niace.org.uk

Support 4 Learning
Resources for advisers, students and all those involved in education, training and communities.
www.support4learning.org.uk

The British Sports Trust
The Trust runs Sports Leaders Awards to enable young people and adults to communicate, organise activities, understand teamwork and motivate others through sport. www.bst.org.uk

The Media Trust
The Media Trust helps voluntary and not-for-profit organisations with their public relations, press, marketing, design, online media and video.
www.mediatrust.co.uk

Tourist Boards
The English, Welsh and Scottish Tourist Boards have websites with lots of ideas for leisure activities.
www.visitengland.com
www.visitwales.com
www.visitscotland.com

The National Trust
Activities, events, ideas and opportunities can be found at www.nationaltrust.org.uk